The End of Days

D1280342

East Meadow Public Library

East Meadow, New York

516-794-2570

www.eastmeadow.info

Books in the
SkyLight Illuminations Series

Bhagavad Gita: Annotated & Explained
The Book of Mormon: Selections Annotated & Explained
Dhammapada: Annotated & Explained
The Divine Feminine in Biblical Wisdom Literature:
*   Selections Annotated & Explained*
Gnostic Writings on the Soul: Annotated & Explained
The End of Days: Essential Selections from Apocalyptic Texts—
*   Annotated & Explained*
Ethics of the Sages: Pirke Avot—*Annotated & Explained*
The Gospel of Philip: Annotated & Explained
The Gospel of Thomas: Annotated & Explained
Hasidic Tales: Annotated & Explained
The Hebrew Prophets: Selections Annotated & Explained
The Hidden Gospel of Matthew: Annotated & Explained
The Lost Sayings of Jesus: Teachings from Ancient Christian, Jewish,
*   Gnostic, and Islamic Sources—Annotated & Explained*
Native American Stories of the Sacred: Annotated & Explained
Philokalia: The Eastern Christian Spiritual Texts—Selections
*   Annotated & Explained*
The Qur'an and Sayings of Prophet Muhammad: Selections
*   Annotated & Explained*
Rumi and Islam: Selections from His Stories, Poems, and Discourses—
*   Annotated & Explained*
The Secret Book of John: The Gnostic Gospel—Annotated & Explained
The Sacred Writings of Paul: Selections Annotated & Explained
Selections from the Gospel of Sri Ramakrishna: Annotated & Explained
Sex Texts from the Bible: Selections Annotated & Explained
Spiritual Writings on Mary: Annotated & Explained
Tao Te Ching: Annotated & Explained
The Way of a Pilgrim: Annotated & Explained
Zohar: Annotated & Explained

The End of Days

Essential Selections from Apocalyptic Texts— Annotated & Explained

Annotation by Robert G. Clouse

Walking Together, Finding the Way ®

Woodstock, Vermont

The End of Days:
Essential Selections from Apocalyptic Texts—Annotated & Explained

2007 First Printing
Annotation and introductory material © 2007 by Robert G. Clouse

Library of Congress Cataloging-in-Publication Data
The end of days : essential selections from apocalyptic texts : annotated & explained / annota-tion by Robert G. Clouse.
    p. cm. — (SkyLight illuminations series)
  Includes bibliographical references.
  ISBN-13: 978-1-59473-170-9
  ISBN-10: 1-59473-170-5
  1. Millennialism—History of doctrines—Sources. 2. End of the world—History of doc-trines—Sources. 3. Bible. N.T. Revelation—Criticism, interpretation, etc.—History—Sources. I. Clouse, Robert G., 1931–

BT892.E53 2007
236'.9—dc22

                                                                              2006101380

10   9   8   7   6   5   4   3   2   1

Manufactured in the United States of America
Cover design: Walter C. Bumford III
Cover art: original image "Black Rider" © Jiri Snaidr, courtesy of www.istockphoto.com, modified by Jenny Buono

SkyLight Paths Publishing is creating a place where people of different spiritual tradi-tions come together for challenge and inspiration, a place where we can help each other understand the mystery that lies at the heart of our existence.

SkyLight Paths sees both believers and seekers as a community that increasingly tran-scends traditional boundaries of religion and denomination—people wanting to learn from each other, *walking together, finding the way.*

SkyLight Paths, "Walking Together, Finding the Way" and colophon are trademarks of LongHill Partners, Inc., registered in the U.S. Patent and Trademark Office.

Walking Together, Finding the Way®
Published by SkyLight Paths® Publishing
A Division of LongHill Partners, Inc.
Sunset Farm Offices, Route 4, P.O. Box 237
Woodstock, VT 05091
Tel: (802) 457-4000   Fax: (802) 457-4004
www.skylightpaths.com

I would like to dedicate this volume to the following individuals who helped me in ways too numerous to mention:

Bonnidell Clouse
Jackie Heighton
Chris Olsen
Steve and Mickey Morahn

And to my patient editors:

Mark Ogilbee and Maura Shaw

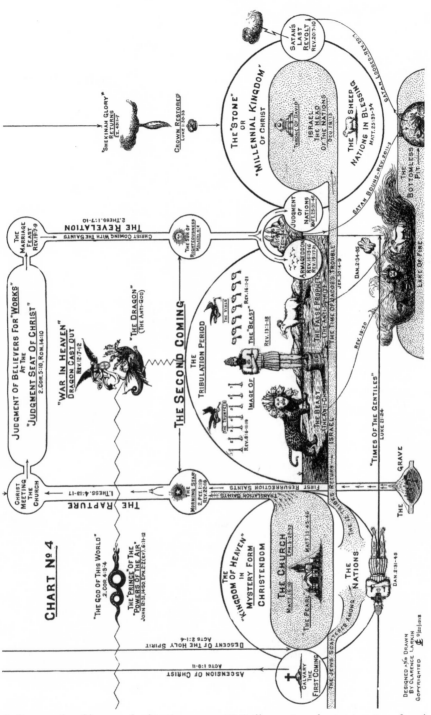

A diagram by Clarence Larkin (see page 154) illustrating the intricacies of end times teachings. Such visual aids were immensely popular at one time.

Contents ☐

Introduction □

We have no evidence that there exists a special sense or ability to perceive future events in the way that we have the senses of sight, touch, hearing, taste, or smell. Yet the future and what it might have in store seems to be a source of endless fascination for us. From the prophecies of the French Renaissance physician Nostradamus to the cycles of the Mayan calendar that ends (and restarts) on December 21, 2012, we speculate, and worry, about what will happen tomorrow.

A class of literature called apocalyptic, which is found in the Hebrew and Christian scriptures as well as in noncanonical sources, deals with this mysterious aspect of human longing. The term comes from the Greek word *apocalypsis*, meaning "unveiling" or "revealing"—as in revealing a secret. The book of Daniel and the book of Revelation in the Bible are the clearest examples of this type of writing, although there are many other examples of literature from the Jewish and Christian traditions that can be classified as Apocalypses.

What makes a particular work an Apocalypse? Apocalypses are stories that use symbols and visions to describe how people received an understanding of future realities from heavenly beings. These visions often describe the meaning of human history and tell of God's judgment on humanity. They usually express the hope of the coming of the kingdom of God to earth and a restoration of idealized, Edenic conditions. An important feature of an Apocalypse is God's judgment—a final confrontation between the forces of good and evil in which evil is defeated forever and God brings about a world ruled by justice and mercy (Rev. 20–22).

The knowledge of these events is communicated to special servants of God by visions, dreams, and angelic messages whose truth and meaning become clear as time passes. Mysterious numbers and strange animal symbols that represent various earthly powers and events are often used. Many parts of the Bible contain elements of apocalyptic writing. Sometimes the visions God gives are interpreted by inspired persons such as Joseph in Genesis 40 and 41. At other times, whole groups of people are affected, as when the inhabitants of Jerusalem are enlightened by the eight visions of Zechariah (Zech. 1–6).

Today, "prophecy" or "Bible prophecy" is often used as a synonym or shorthand for such apocalyptic visions and predictions, but this is an unfortunate label that does a disservice to those interested in the multidimensional complexity of the Bible's prophetic words. In the Bible, apocalyptic passages are not necessarily the same as prophetic passages. Although the inspired prophets of Israel delivered messages that God gave them, predicting the future was but one characteristic of their messages. Their prophesying was more challenging and, some would argue, more radical than merely foretelling future events; their messages were also powerful challenges and stern warnings to people in their own day to purify religious worship and to help the poor and oppressed. The gravity of their messages lay not in a distant fulfillment of some curious vision, but in the speaking of truth to power in their own time and place.

Indeed, it has been said that when powerful prophetic words decline, Apocalypse arises, and so it was in the second century B.C.E. through the second century C.E. During those years, it was evident that the prophetic tradition that had dominated the religious and moral life of Israel for centuries had ceased, and apocalyptic literature, some of which is preserved in the Bible, became especially prominent. More liberal interpreters tend to date such biblical passages to this time frame, believing that those who wrote apocalyptic books then attributed them to earlier individuals such as Daniel to lend their writings credibility—a common and accepted practice in the ancient world. Conservative scholars, on the other hand, do not believe it is necessary to date the apocalyptic passages scattered throughout the Bible (see Isa. 6, 24, 1 Kings 22, Eze. 1–2, 8, 12–14, 38–39) to this four-century-long time frame.

In any case, in addition to the canonical books with apocalyptic context such as Matthew 24–25, Mark 13, Luke 21, 1 Thessalonians 4:13–18, Daniel, and Revelation, there are also Jewish and Christian Apocalypses not included in the Hebrew Bible or the New Testament, such as I Enoch, 4 Ezra, 2 and 3 Baruch, Apocalypse of Peter, Shepherd of Hermas, and the Ascension of Isaiah.

Jesus also used apocalyptic texts and references in his explanation of the kingdom of God, and the apostle Paul in his preaching to Gentile audiences emphasized the imminent end of the world that was to be accomplished by the second coming of Christ. Most biblical scholars have given these apocalyptic symbols and visions vague interpretations indicating that they are meant to give hope to Christians in times of crisis. By seeing that God is in control of events and has a plan for history, God's people are encouraged to look beyond death toward a time of universal justice under divine control.

Others, however, have not been satisfied with the vague interpretations of these scholars and have focused instead on precise interpretations of key passages such as Revelation 20:1–6, which describes a thousand-year-long kingdom, usually called the millennium, when Christ will reign upon earth and the forces of evil will be restrained.[1]

Categories of Interpretation

Particular interpretations of this coming millennium have varied throughout history, but each tends to fall into one of three categories that have historically been called premillennial, postmillennial, and amillennial.[2] These categories continue in use despite the fact that the distinction involves much more than merely whether Christ returns before (pre-) or after (post-) the millennium, or whether there will be a literal millennium at all (a-). The kingdom expected by postmillennialists is quite different from that anticipated by premillennialists, not only with respect to the time and manner with which it will be established but also with regard to the nature of the kingdom and the way Christ exercises his control over it. Postmillennialists (also known as postmillenarians) believe that the kingdom of God is extended through Christian preaching and teaching, as a result of which the world will be Christianized and will enjoy a long period of peace and righteousness. This new age will not be essentially different from the present, and it will emerge gradually as an ever-larger share of the world's population is converted to Christianity. Evil will not be eliminated but will be reduced to a minimum as the moral and spiritual influence of Christianity is heightened. During this age, the church will assume a greater importance, and many social, economic, and educational problems will be solved. The period will close with the second coming of Christ, the resurrection of the dead, and the final judgment.[3]

By contrast, amillennialists believe that the Bible does not predict a period of universal peace and righteousness before the end of the world. There will not be an actual reign of Christ upon the earth, nor will there be a long period of ever-increasing peace and prosperity. Instead, such passages from the Bible are to be understood spiritually and metaphorically, for good and evil will coexist right up until the second coming of Christ, when the dead are raised and the last judgment held.[4]

The third major interpretation, premillennialism, is also the most intricate and the one with the longest history. It affirms that the Lord will return suddenly, an event that will be followed by the millennial thousand-year period of peace and righteousness, during which Christ will reign as king in person or through a select group of people. This kingdom is not established by the conversion of individual souls over a long period of time, but suddenly and by overwhelming power from heaven. In this new age, Jews will be converted to Christianity, and all of nature will be in such harmony that the desert will blossom like a rose and even ferocious beasts will be tamed. Evil will be held in check during this period by the reigning Christ, who will rule with a rod of iron. Many premillennialists believe that during this golden age believers who have died will be reunited with glorified bodies to mingle freely with the rest of the inhabitants of the earth.

Yet, despite these idyllic conditions, people will not be satisfied, and at the end of the thousand years some will launch one last rebellion against

God and his followers. This final exposure of evil will be crushed by Christ and then the last judgment will be held, which will give way to eternal bliss or damnation.

A telling characteristic of premillennialism is the teaching that the return of Christ will be preceded by certain signs, such as the preaching of the gospel to all nations, a great apostasy, wars, famine, earthquakes, the appearance of the Antichrist, and a great tribulation.[5] Hence, many premillennialists attempt to read the signs of the times—with the Bible in one hand and a newspaper in the other, to paraphrase an old saying—seeing in current events the fulfillment of biblical prophecies that point to Christ's reappearing.

Despite the usefulness of these three categories, it is important to remember that they are not wholly adequate and can lead to inaccurate generalizations. For example, it is often stated that postmillennialism is an extremely optimistic creed that is little more than a Christian blessing on the secular teaching that humankind will progress to some utopian social goal. In reality, many of the most fervent evangelicals have taken a postmillennial view, believing that the Holy Spirit can bring a great revival to the world. This outlook has encouraged them to preach the gospel with great fervency and led to global evangelism and missionary work. It is even possible to be a pessimistic postmillennialist, that is, one who believes the immediate future holds a time of trouble for the church, but that God will send his Spirit in a special way to overcome these problems.

Premillennialism in particular is also a more difficult doctrine to define than it would seem at first glance. Not all premillennialists are consistent; for instance, some have decided in ages past to actually prepare the way for the coming of Christ by force if necessary, an approach not shared with most of their premillennial brethren. For another example, many premillenarians believe that the Jews will be restored to their land and Jerusalem will be the center of the millennial state, but this has not been followed by all who hold to a premillennial advent. In fact, one leading Puritan millennial scholar believed that America would be the center of Christ's kingdom.[6]

Yet another difference that confuses the usual categories of eschatological interpretation is whether the book of Revelation, which forms the backbone of these theories, is interpreted in a preterist, historicist, or futurist manner. A preterist is one who believes that most of the prophecies of Revelation, sometimes called simply the Apocalypse, have been fulfilled in the past. The historicist (or presentist) considers the events of Revelation now in the process of fulfillment, and the futurist believes that the bulk of the book refers to events yet to come. Until the nineteenth century, most premillennialists used the historicist method of interpretation—they believed that the prophecies of Revelation were being fulfilled before their very eyes. Today the usual premillennial emphasis is futurist—we are not yet seeing their fulfillment, but will, and that right soon.

Nevertheless, despite these qualifications, these broad categories of premillennial, postmillennial, and amillennial interpretations concerning the second coming of Christ remain useful descriptions for study, if for no other reason than they are still so widely used.[7]

Millennialism in the Early Christian Era

In each era of church history, including the ancient, medieval, Reformation, and modern periods, one of these views has tended to predominate. During the first three centuries of the Christian era, premillennialism was the prevailing interpretation. The first postapostolic writer to express the premillenarian faith was Papias, a bishop of Hierapolis in Phrygia. He described the golden age of the personal rule of Christ upon earth as characterized by miracles and natural blessings. Not only would the earth yield abundant crops, but peaceful relations would be established among animals and humans. His belief was based upon combining Hebrew Bible texts with Revelation 20. Irenaeus, Justin Martyr, Tertullian, Hippolytus, Methodius, Commodianus, and Lactantius also kept the apostolic witness to premillennialism alive.

When Emperor Constantine legalized Christianity, much of the impetus for millennial teaching passed. Premillennialism thrives when Christians are persecuted or feel themselves pressured by society, but during the fourth century official hostility was replaced by government support for the church. An alternative view of the millennium had already been developed in Alexandria by scholars such as Origen (d. 254). His nonliteral approach to the scriptures asserted that the Christian hope was to be in heaven, not on earth, and that believers should take a spiritual interpretation of the book of Revelation.

This amillennialism of the Alexandrine theologians, which was expanded by Tyconius, a little-known Donatist writer of the late fourth century, was later adopted by the medieval church because of its acceptance by the prestigious Church Father Augustine (354–430). Early in his career, Augustine had held a millenarian view, but due to the exaggerations and crude materialism of many chiliasts (premillennialists), he abandoned the teaching in favor of a spiritualized and metaphorical interpretation of apocalyptic texts. Hence, the "first resurrection" of the saints described in Revelation was not literal, but figurative, and represented the conversion experience; and the thousand years were also symbolic, standing for the Christian era or church age. Thus, Augustine propounded the doctrine demanded by the times and, by applying an allegorical interpretation, believed that the millennium was realized in the church.

The Medieval Period

For the next 1,300 years, Augustinian amillennialism remained the official teaching of the church. However, during the medieval period there was always an undercurrent of premillennialism among certain leaders and factions, including Joachim of Fiora and the Spiritual Franciscans.[8] In the fourteenth and fifteenth centuries, their teaching was revived by various pre-Reformation groups, including the Hussites.[9] However, the Protestant Reformers of the sixteenth century continued to hold the Augustinian view of the millennium; nevertheless they suggested changes in eschatological interpretation that led to a renewal of premillennialism in the seventeenth century. Martin Luther, for example, advocated a more literal approach to the Bible and identified the papacy with the Antichrist, and the attention that he called to the prophetic portions of the Bible led some Lutheran scholars to adopt a millennialist interpretation.[10]

John Calvin, like Luther, was not impressed with millenarian interpretation, possibly because of the activities of certain radical premillennialist groups such as the Munster Anabaptists. Their bloody methods of trying to establish Christ's reign on earth for him led to the first official condemnation of millennialism in sixteenth-century Protestant creeds, such as the Second Helvetic Confession of the Reformed Churches, and in an early version of the Articles of Religion of the Church of England.[11] Nevertheless, a German Calvinist—despite Calvin's opposition—named Johann H. Alsted (1588–1638), revived the teaching of premillennialism, putting it in a more respectable form.[12]

Alsted's work was adopted by a learned Anglican scholar, Joseph Mede (1586–1638), who popularized the premillennial view in the English-speaking world. Mede, called by some the greatest biblical scholar the Anglican Church has ever produced, was deeply influential to the course of premillennial interpretation. He considered that his great advance in the interpretation of prophecy was his discovery of the "synchronism" of prophecies. By that he meant that many of the prophetic teachings scattered throughout the book of Revelation actually recapitulated the same (future) time period and describe different beings or events during that time.

Moreover, Mede thought that he was living in the midst of that very time period when the prophecies were being fulfilled. His application of apocalyptic passages to his own historical milieu continues to be virtually the de rigueur approach among each successive generation of devotees to premillennialist teachings.

Not surprisingly, Mede's work was extremely popular, both in his own day and in the decades that followed. During the Puritan Revolution of the seventeenth century, his ideas helped fan the fire of prophetic enthusiasm. Despite the radical action of groups like English religious and political agitators the Fifth Monarchy Men, who helped discredit premillennial belief, there were always individuals of great influence, such as Isaac Newton, who followed Mede's ideas. Many Bible students in colonial America, including Cotton Mather, were impressed by the theology of the "great Mede" and followed the ideas of the English scholar.

Postmillennialism in the Eighteenth Century

Although premillennialism continued, it was destined to be eclipsed by postmillennialism during the eighteenth century. Postmillennialism was expressed by Daniel Whitby (1638–1725), who formulated a teaching that can be found in the works of earlier seventeenth-century Puritan writers. An Anglican latitudinarian, he published the two-volume *Paraphrase and Commentary on the New Testament*, to which he appended, in place of a commentary on the Revelation, an essay titled *A Treatise of the True Millennium: Showing that it is not a reign of Persons Raised from the Dead, but of the Church flourishing Gloriously for a Thousand years after the conversion of the Jews, and the Flowing in of all nations to them thus converted to the Christian faith*. Whitby, as his cumbersome title indicates, believed that the Jews would be converted to Christianity and that this would result in the beginning of the millennium. The golden age was to be a time of ease and plenty, universal peace, freedom from persecution, righteousness, and the special presence of God on earth. He felt that this would be the result of a fresh outpouring of the Holy Spirit as at the day of Pentecost in the book of Acts. He did not teach a literal appearance of Christ on earth or a resurrection of the dead before the millennium.

During the eighteenth century, Whitby's eschatology proved to be very popular. Two writers of popular commentaries on Revelation, Charles Daubuz and Moses Lowman, both espoused the postmillennial view.[13] One of the most influential American theologians who ever lived, Jonathan Edwards, also adopted this outlook. Millennial considerations were more important to Edwards than has often been realized. In fact, he kept a notebook on the Apocalypse that spans nearly three decades of his life.[14] In this work he not only analyzed the book and kept notes on commentators on the Revelation, but he also recorded the signs of the times that he believed were leading to the millennium. Other works that he wrote dealing with this millennial enthusiasm are *A History of Redemption (1774)* and *Some thoughts concerning the Present Revival of Religion in New England (1743)*. In these books, Edwards confesses his belief that there will be a golden age for the church on earth achieved through the ordinary process of preaching the gospel in the power of the Holy Spirit. The Protestant Reformation had begun this process by undermining the power of the papacy, which Edwards identified as the Antichrist. A great outpouring of the Holy Spirit would finally destroy the Antichrist, and as a result Satan's visible kingdom, the apostate church, would be overthrown and a great age of human happiness would follow. During this time heresy, infidelity, and superstition would be eliminated. Islam would be destroyed, the Jews converted, and the heathen of Africa, America, and India won to Christ. The millennial age was to be characterized not only by great holiness and commitment to Christ but also by a vast increase in knowledge and learning. The reign of Christ would result in international peace and understanding accompanied by the greatest prosperity and happiness the world has ever experienced. In addition to all these impressive blessings, it would be a time when Christianity and the church will be greatly respected.

At the close of the millennial age, however, much of the world would fall away from Christ and his church. Vast numbers would be recruited into the mighty armies of Gog and Magog, an end-times military coalition arrayed against God as foretold by the Hebrew prophet Ezekiel, because people abused the prosperity of the era to serve lust and corruption. Christ then would come and crush this rebellion, instituting the last judgment, after which the church would be caught up in the clouds to meet the Lord in the air and the world would be set on fire, becoming a great furnace where all the enemies of Christ would be tormented forever.

The Modern Era

Just as the influence of Augustine had led the medieval church to adopt amillennialism, so the teaching of Edwards encouraged the spread of postmillennialism in the modern era. However, there were still individuals who preached premillennialism, and by the early nineteenth century their number increased because of a renewal of interest in prophecy fostered by the French Revolution. When the French overthrew their monarch in 1789, Europe was plunged into decades of turbulence that encouraged apocalyptic thinking. The Revolution caused the destruction of papal power in France, the seizure of church property, the founding of a religion of reason, and even for a time the banishment of the pope from Rome. Students of prophecy believed that this "deadly wound" inflicted on the papacy was prophesied in Revelation 13. Most of these interpreters believed that the papacy must be destroyed before the millennium would come, and many Bible scholars in Britain came to the conclusion that the end of the age was near. Biblical chronology seemed to point to the late eighteenth and early nineteenth centuries as the decisive period for the establishment of the millennium.

The new prophetic movement centered in Britain, where a vast literature on millennial themes developed in the first half of the nineteenth century. Most of these writers were from the Church of England and the Presbyterian Church of Scotland. Those who led the movement became convinced of the premillennial return of Jesus Christ. They also had a great interest in the conversion of the Jews to Christ and their restoration to the Holy Land. By 1826, Henry Drummond, an influential politician and businessman, had become interested in the conversion of the Jews and the Bible prophecies relating to the second coming of Christ. In that year, he held a series of prophecy conferences at his estate attended by several important laymen and ministers. These meetings were repeated in 1826 and 1828.

Many Americans went to Britain, where they were caught up in the enthusiasm about the return of Christ. One of these, Eleazar Lord (1788–1871), was a prominent businessman who, with his brother David (1792–1880), began to popularize premillennialism in the United States. Eleazar's money and David's erudition and energy made a formidable combination. David wrote numerous books, edited an important theological journal, and rose to prominence among premillennialists by systematizing their doctrine to an extent never before attempted. He set forth rules for the literal method of interpretation so that among many American premillennials there was an agreed-upon standard for prophetic analysis. The suggestions that he made include a careful distinction between "language prophecies" and "symbolical prophecies." The former should conform to the laws of language and grammar, which he enumerates for his readers, whereas the latter "were, with few exceptions, revealed to the prophet in dreams or visions."[15] He believed that his method, if used consistently, would stop postmillennial interpretations.

Using these principles, Lord proceeded to elaborate a premillennial system based upon the historicist interpretation of the book of Revelation, which held that biblical prophecies were in the process of being fulfilled. Yet he states bluntly at the beginning of one of his books that humankind as a whole is not to be redeemed under the present dispensation, or era. Rather it is a period of trial when men and women choose between good and evil and show whether they follow God or not. Mocking the idea of worldwide revival, he felt that the optimism of the postmillennialists could be disproved from scriptures such as John 16:32–33, Acts 14:22, and 1 Thessalonians 3:3–4, which picture the present age as a time of trial and discipline in which evil and good are tested and made to reveal themselves. The purpose of the present age was to prepare the way for another dispensation, during which the world could be redeemed and salvation extended to all nations. That dispensation would begin, Lord taught, when Christ returned to inaugurate the millennium and to reign in person.

Lord's system won many followers, not only among his fellow New England Calvinists but also among other groups. These premillenarian believers would be found in such major denominations as the Lutheran (Joseph Seiss), Episcopalian (R. C. Shimeall), Methodist (John G. Wilson), Baptist (James Inglis), and Dutch Reformed churches (John Demarest), as well as the Congregational and Presbyterian churches. Yet the hostility of many of these main denominations forced premillennialists to create their own structures. This trend reached its fruition when millenarian conferences were held in the 1870s.

In addition to these national meetings there were local prophecy assemblies, such as the Premillennial Advent Society of New York City as well as several Jewish societies in the leading eastern communities. The formation of these new groups indicates that one had to depart from the general tenor of American life to adopt the premillennial view. Chiliasts held a special set of doctrines and subscribed to a rather well-defined theology, including a literal approach to the scriptures, two resurrections of the saints, and the restoration of the Jews to the Holy Land. End times scholar Robert K. Whalen has noted, "By 1860, millenarianism had emerged so clearly as a peculiar theology that its proponents formed virtually a sect within the larger body of American Protestantism. Like the red thread which the British admiralty used to weave into its cordage to identify it as its own, millenarianism ran through various denominations, part of the whole, but always a self-identifying thing apart."[16]

Premillennialism, because it was a well-articulated theology with considerable structure and a defined leadership, was equipped to last and develop as one of the main ingredients of the fundamentalist movement that emerged at the dawn of the twentieth century.

The Twentieth Century

Despite the success of the historicist movement, a new type of premillennialism called dispensationalism was to be prominent in the twentieth century. John Nelson Darby, an early leader of an English millennialist sect known as the Plymouth Brethren, articulated the dispensationalist understanding of prophecy, which took a futurist view of prophetic fulfillment. Through a series of books, which include four volumes on prophecy, his ideas became popular in the English-speaking world. The line of continuity from Darby can be traced through popular Bible preachers and teachers right to the present time. Dispensationalism has become the standard interpretation for dozens of Bible institutes and seminaries in the United States. Many famous interdenominational evangelists, including D. L. Moody and Billy Graham, have also adopted this understanding of eschatology. Periodicals and books such as the phenomenal best sellers *The Late Great Planet Earth* and the *Left Behind* series have also popularized this approach.[17]

As the name suggests, dispensationalists believe that God deals with humanity through a series of distinct periods. Although they differ on the exact numbers of these eras, most believe that there are seven dispensations: innocence, conscience or moral responsibility, human government, promise, the law, the church, and the millennium. In each of these ages there is a unique revelation of the divine will, and humankind is tested by obedience to this standard. The seventh dispensation, the millennium, will be inaugurated by the return of Christ in two stages: the first, a secret rapture that removes the church before the great tribulation devastates the earth; and the second, Christ's coming with the church to establish the kingdom.

The Jews have a prominent place in these events, and by the time the millennium is established most of them will be converted to Christ. During the millennial age the resurrected saints will rule the world with their Lord. Peace and prosperity will come to earth, and worship will center in the rebuilt temple in Jerusalem. At the beginning of the millennium, only believers will be alive, but some of their descendants will not accept Christ and they will join Satan in a revolt against God. This final example of human depravity will be defeated by divine intervention, the last judgment will be held, and the eternal state of heaven and hell will be established.[18] As previously suggested, this interpretation of the millennial hope is currently the most widely held premillennial view.

In summary, throughout the history of the church, each interpretation of the Christian hope has had its share of adherents. During the first three centuries, premillennialism seems to have predominated. Beginning in the fifth century with the teaching of the Church Father Augustine, amillennialism dominated the medieval church. The seventeenth century witnessed a revival of premillennialism and the emergence of postmillennialism. Due to the prestige of scholars such as Jonathan Edwards, postmillennialism prevailed and continued its popularity until the early nineteenth century. By the twentieth century, a new form of premillennialism, dispensationalism, became the major interpretation of those who emphasized the second coming of Christ.[19]

Despite the extravagant claims of some of its followers, premillennialism continues to be the most vital apocalyptic interpretation. In every age when the return of Christ has been a living hope for the believer, premillennialism has been the prevailing view. Even today it is among dispensationalists that the second coming is emphasized. Those who adopt other views seldom mention the return of Christ or that history will end one day with the establishment of God's kingdom. Yet as the popular conservative writer C. S. Lewis has so well described, the doctrine of the Lord's return in all its varieties can be a powerful source of hope and comfort: "Frantic administration of panaceas to the world is certainly discouraged by the reflection that 'this present' might be 'the world's last night'; sober work for the future, within the limits of ordinary morality and prudence, is not. For what comes is Judgment: happy are those whom it finds laboring in their vocations, whether they were merely going out to feed the pigs or laying good plans to deliver humanity a hundred years hence from some great evil. The curtain has indeed now fallen. Those pigs will never in fact be fed, the great campaign against White Slavery or Governmental tyranny will never in fact proceed to victory. No matter; you were at your post when the Inspection came."[20]

The End of Days

◆ Although most Christians have historically denied the practice of setting specific dates for the return of Christ, the belief that his reappearance is imminent—that he could return at any time—has persisted throughout the ages. In the current-day dispensational evangelical framework, this belief is frequently bolstered by identifying a series of events described in the Bible as they will unfold in the end days. The timeline for these events is often patterned on a period of seventy weeks as envisioned by the Hebrew prophet Daniel.

1 In this scheme, the seventy weeks are understood to be symbolic, with each "week" consisting of seven years; one of Daniel's prophetic weeks, therefore, equals seven years in human history. At the end of the seventy prophetic weeks, all struggle will cease and God's people will be brought into "everlasting righteousness."

2 The seventy weeks—and the prophetic clock—began in the sixth century B.C.E. with the decree to rebuild the temple in Jerusalem under Ezra and Nehemiah, a process associated with seven of Daniel's weeks (49 years).

3 Sixty-two weeks (434 years) after the rebuilding of the temple, the Messiah was to come and subsequently be "cut off"—understood to be a prediction of Christ's birth and crucifixion. With Christ's (first) appearance on earth, Daniel's prophetic clock paused and today, some two thousand years later, the clock is still on hold. We are in a limbo state between the sixty-ninth and seventieth weeks of Daniel's prophecy.

4 When the clock begins ticking again, Daniel's seventieth week will commence and the Antichrist will arise and hold sway over the earth for that week—for seven years. In that time he will "confirm the covenant"—allow the Jews to restore their covenantal temple rites—but "in the midst of the week" (that is, after three and a half years) he will renege on his promise, initiating a time of unimaginable calamity and suffering upon the world. After another three and a half years, the prophetic clock will run out, and the time of "everlasting righteousness" mentioned at the beginning of the passage will begin.

1 □ Biblical Foundations

The Seventy Weeks of Years

Seventy weeks[1] are determined upon thy people and upon thy holy city, to finish the transgression, and to make an end of sins, and to make reconciliation for iniquity, and to bring in everlasting righteousness, and to seal up the vision and prophecy, and to anoint the most Holy. Know therefore and understand, *that* from the going forth of the commandment to restore and to build Jerusalem[2] unto the Messiah the Prince *shall be* seven weeks, and threescore and two weeks: the street shall be built again, and the wall, even in troublous times. And after threescore and two weeks shall Messiah be cut off, [3] but not for himself: and the people of the prince that shall come shall destroy the city and the sanctuary; and the end thereof *shall be* with a flood, and unto the end of the war desolations are determined. And he shall confirm the covenant with many for one week: and in the midst of the week he shall cause the sacrifice and the oblation to cease, and for the overspreading of abominations he shall make *it* desolate, even until the consummation, and that determined shall be poured upon the desolate.[4]

—DANIEL 9:24–27

◆ Using Daniel's seventy weeks as a skeletal outline, many prophecy-minded teachers turn to other biblical passages and extrapolate details to stitch together a pastiche of what those final days will entail. This is particularly true of dispensationalists, whose method of interpreting the Bible allows for such a unity of purpose among a variety of texts. Following is a more detailed generalized understanding, from such a dispensational premillennialist perspective, of the sequence of events that will accompany Christ's return, and biblical passages commonly used to support it.

5 One of the signs heralding the end times is the supposed apostasy of the larger Christian denominations. These verses call to mind certain practices of the Roman Catholic Church, a common target for accusations of end-times apostasy.

6 This is another passage often used to identify established denominations as portents of the end. Part of the fascination of apocalyptic teaching for many individuals is the anticlerical sentiment found here. It is always easy to point out the inconsistencies and shortcomings of larger, more ordered religious organizations and thus give a prophetic legitimacy to independent schismatic groups that follow prophetic teaching.

Increase in Apostasy

Now the Spirit speaketh expressly, that in the latter times some shall depart from the faith, giving heed to seducing spirits, and doctrines of devils; Speaking lies in hypocrisy; having their conscience seared with a hot iron; Forbidding to marry, *and commanding* to abstain from meats, which God hath created to be received with thanksgiving of them which believe and know the truth.[5]

—1 TIMOTHY 4:1–3

This know also, that in the last days perilous times shall come. For men shall be lovers of their own selves, covetous, boasters, proud, blasphemers, disobedient to parents, unthankful, unholy, Without natural affection, trucebreakers, false accusers, incontinent, fierce, despisers of those that are good, Traitors, heady, highminded, lovers of pleasures more than lovers of God; Having a form of godliness, but denying the power thereof: from such turn away.[6]

—2 TIMOTHY 3:1–5

7 Since dispensationalists make a definite distinction between God's program for Israel and his program for the church, they believe the church will be removed from the earth so that Israel's destiny may be fulfilled. This event, commonly called the rapture (the translation of the Greek word *parousia* in 1 Thess. 4:17), marks the end of "the times of the Gentiles," which Jesus mentioned in Luke 21:24. During the rapture, believers will be caught up (or taken up) from the earth to meet Christ in the air. The unbelieving world will not see this take place, but they will witness its effects—the sudden and mysterious disappearance of many people.

This is the blessed hope of the believer and is something that can happen at any time. No preconditions exist that require the Lord to delay coming for his church. He will come suddenly, like a thief in the night. Those believers who are alive at the time will be translated, that is, their bodies will be perfected, a condition that will be theirs throughout all eternity. At the same moment, those saints who have already died in Christ will be resurrected and will join the living believers as they proceed upward to meet their Lord in the air. The rapture heralds a chain of events that will mark the beginning of a seven-year period known as the tribulation—the final week of Daniel's seventy weeks of years.

8 Then all Christians will appear before the judgment seat of Christ and will be rewarded for the good works they have accomplished on earth. All unbelievers will remain behind and will go through the tribulation period, the time when the wrath of God will be poured out on the earth (1 Thess. 1:10).

9 A minority of dispensationalists hold to variant positions concerning the rapture. Some believe that only those who are faithful and watching will be called up. Those careless Christians who are indifferent to his return will go through the tribulation.

The Rapture

But I would not have you to be ignorant, brethren, concerning them which are asleep, that ye sorrow not, even as others which have no hope. For if we believe that Jesus died and rose again, even so them also which sleep in Jesus will God bring with him. For this we say unto you by the word of the Lord, that we which are alive *and* remain unto the coming of the Lord shall not prevent them which are asleep. For the Lord himself shall descend from heaven with a shout, with the voice of the archangel, and with the trump of God: and the dead in Christ shall rise first: Then we which are alive *and* remain shall be caught up together with them in the clouds, to meet the Lord in the air: and so shall we ever be with the Lord. Wherefore comfort one another with these words.[7]

—1 THESSALONIANS 4:13–18

For we must all appear before the judgment seat of Christ; that every one may receive the things *done* in *his* body, according to that he hath done, whether *it be* good or bad.[8]

—2 CORINTHIANS 5:10

So Christ was once offered to bear the sins of many; and unto them that look for him shall he appear the second time without sin unto salvation.[9]

—HEBREWS 9:28

10 Another view is that the rapture occurs midway through the tribulation period. The trumpet will sound after three and a half years, that is, in the middle of the great tribulation. Yet another position is that the church will go through the tribulation and receive supernatural protection from Christ. The saints will go to meet their Lord just before the second coming.

11 Once the church has been raptured, Daniel's prophetic clock will start up again and begin counting down the final prophetic week of seven years. The Holy Spirit will remove his restraining hand, and all hell will literally break loose on earth. The preeminent world power will be a revived Roman Empire consisting of a ten-nation confederacy led by a ruthless king who even before the rapture will have been crushing his associates in an effort to establish absolute rule. Many believe that, in all probability, the United States will be aligned with the new Rome.

12 The ruler of the empire, who is called the "beast" in Revelation 13, is also portrayed as the "man of lawlessness" and the Antichrist. He is the very personification of Satan himself. His seven-year reign will be marked by utter tyranny and incomprehensible horror.

Now this I say, brethren, that flesh and blood cannot inherit the kingdom of God; neither doth corruption inherit incorruption. Behold, I shew you a mystery; We shall not all sleep, but we shall all be changed, In a moment, in the twinkling of an eye, at the last trump: for the trumpet shall sound, and the dead shall be raised incorruptible, and we shall be changed.[10]

—1 Corinthians 15:50–52

The Tribulation

And after threescore and two weeks shall Messiah be cut off, but not for himself: and the people of the prince that shall come shall destroy the city and the sanctuary; and the end thereof *shall be* with a flood, and unto the end of the war desolations are determined.[11]

—Daniel 9:26

And the beast which I saw was like unto a leopard, and his feet were as *the feet* of a bear, and his mouth as the mouth of a lion: and the dragon gave him his power, and his seat, and great authority. And I saw one of his heads as it were wounded to death; and his deadly wound was healed: and all the world wondered after the beast. And they worshipped the dragon which gave power unto the beast: and they worshipped the beast, saying, Who *is* like unto the beast? who is able to make war with him? ... And he opened his mouth in blasphemy against God, to blaspheme his name, and his tabernacle, and them that dwell in heaven. And it was given unto him to make war with the saints, and to overcome them: and power was given him over all kindreds, and tongues, and nations. And all that dwell upon the earth shall worship him, whose names are not written in the book of life of the Lamb slain from the foundation of the world. If any man have an ear, let him hear.[12]

—Revelation 13:2–4, 6–9

13 The Antichrist's activity will center around a relationship that he will establish with the newly restored nation of Israel. The Antichrist and Israel will work out a diplomatic agreement that permits the Jews to reconstruct the temple and restore their sacrificial system, and he will move his capital to Jerusalem. However, three and a half years after signing the treaty, the Antichrist will double-cross his Jewish allies. He will defile the temple by entering it, even though he is a Gentile, and will order the immediate suspension of the sacrifices.

14 The Antichrist will declare that he himself is God and demand the worship of all people on earth. He will be the "abomination that causes desolation" that Jesus describes here in Matthew's Gospel.

◆ The backdrop to the Antichrist's rise to power will be a time of unparalleled destruction, violence, and misery.

And he shall confirm the covenant with many for one week: and in the midst of the week he shall cause the sacrifice and the oblation to cease, and for the overspreading of abominations he shall make *it* desolate, even until the consummation, and that determined shall be poured upon the desolate.[13]

—DANIEL 9:27

And as [Jesus] sat upon the mount of Olives, the disciples came unto him privately, saying, Tell us, when shall these things be? and what *shall be* the sign of thy coming, and of the end of the world? And Jesus answered and said unto them, Take heed that no man deceive you. For many shall come in my name, saying, I am Christ; and shall deceive many. And ye shall hear of wars and rumours of wars: see that ye be not troubled: for all *these things* must come to pass, but the end is not yet. For nation shall rise against nation, and kingdom against kingdom: and there shall be famines, and pestilences, and earthquakes, in divers places. All these *are* the beginning of sorrows. Then shall they deliver you up to be afflicted, and shall kill you: and ye shall be hated of all nations for my name's sake. And then shall many be offended, and shall betray one another, and shall hate one another. And many false prophets shall rise, and shall deceive many. And because iniquity shall abound, the love of many shall wax cold. But he that shall endure unto the end, the same shall be saved. And this gospel of the kingdom shall be preached in all the world for a witness unto all nations; and then shall the end come. When ye therefore shall see the abomination of desolation,[14] spoken of by Daniel the prophet, stand in the holy place, (whoso readeth, let him understand,) then let them which be in Judea flee into the mountains: Let him which is on the housetop not come down to take any thing out of his house: Neither let him which is in the field return back to take his clothes. And woe unto them that are with child, and to them that give suck in those days! But pray ye that your flight be not in the winter, neither on the sabbath day: For then shall be great tribulation, such as was not since the beginning of the world to this time, no, nor ever shall be.

—MATTHEW 24:3–21

15 To carry out his blasphemous demands, the Antichrist will turn to an associate called the false prophet and delegate authority to him to compel all people to worship the beast. He will do this through naked force, the use of miracle-working powers (including a counterfeit resurrection), and economic pressure. The latter is the infamous "mark of the beast," the mysterious symbolic 666, which dispensationalists equate with a world government that will regulate, in a computerized age, all aspects of one's economic and business life. For three and a half years those who refuse to give their allegiance to the Antichrist will be subjected to a reign of terror. During the tribulation, many people will turn to Christ after hearing the gospel message through the preaching of the "two witnesses" (Rev. 11:3–12), and they will be relentlessly persecuted. As believers they will oppose the beast's rule, and as a result, they will not be able to buy or sell goods or hold jobs. They will be hunted down and executed. Only those who have hidden away food and other necessities of life in secret caches will be able to escape the clutches of the beast's enforcers.

And I beheld another beast coming up out of the earth; and he had two horns like a lamb, and he spake as a dragon. And he exerciseth all the power of the first beast before him, and causeth the earth and them which dwell therein to worship the first beast, whose deadly wound was healed. And he doeth great wonders, so that he maketh fire come down from heaven on the earth in the sight of men, And deceiveth them that dwell on the earth by *the means of* those miracles which he had power to do in the sight of the beast; saying to them that dwell on the earth, that they should make an image to the beast, which had the wound by a sword, and did live. And he had power to give life unto the image of the beast, that the image of the beast should both speak, and cause that as many as would not worship the image of the beast should be killed. And he causeth all, both small and great, rich and poor, free and bond, to receive a mark in their right hand, or in their foreheads: And that no man might buy or sell, save he that had the mark, or the name of the beast, or the number of his name. Here is wisdom. Let him that hath understanding count the number of the beast: for it is the number of a man; and his number *is* Six hundred three score *and* six.[15]

—REVELATION 13:11–18

16 Now begins what Jeremiah 30:7 calls "the time of Jacob's trouble." Israel has tied its fate to the deified world dictator, but his reign starts to unravel. Now the four horsemen of the Apocalypse ride forth to bring additional calamity upon the world. The second of these dreaded horsemen, the red horse, is usually associated with the unleashing of war on the earth.

17 In spite of the Antichrist's enormous political power, a few places will remain outside his authority. Thus, an all-out war will break out when a northern confederacy under Russia's leadership, the "king of the north," moves south of Israel in a lightning offensive, hoping to fulfill the dream of both the tsarist and communist rulers of securing control of the Middle East and its vast wealth and resources. Convinced that the Antichrist will not mount an effective defense of the corrupted Jewish state, the Russian leader will join forces with the "king of the south," an Arab-African confederacy, and assault the Antichrist's seat of government in Jerusalem.

18 However, the godless master of Jerusalem will launch a successful counterattack, which in turn will provoke certain "kings of the east."

And I saw when the Lamb opened one of the seals, and I heard, as it were the noise of thunder, one of the four beasts saying, Come and see. And I saw, and behold a white horse: and he that sat on him had a bow; and a crown was given unto him: and he went forth conquering, and to conquer. And when he had opened the second seal, I heard the second beast say, Come and see. And there went out another horse *that was* red: and *power* was given to him that sat thereon to take peace from the earth, and that they should kill one another: and there was given unto him a great sword. And when he had opened the third seal, I heard the third beast say, Come and see. And I beheld, and lo a black horse; and he that sat on him had a pair of balances in his hand. And I heard a voice in the midst of the four beasts say, A measure of wheat for a penny, and three measures of barley for a penny; and *see* thou hurt not the oil and the wine. And when he had opened the fourth seal, I heard the voice of the fourth beast say, Come and see. And I looked and behold a pale horse: and his name that sat on him was Death, and Hell followed with him. And power was given unto them over the fourth part of the earth, to kill with sword, and with hunger, and with death, and with the beasts of the earth.[16]

—REVELATION 6:1–17

And at the time of the end shall the king of the south push at him: and the king of the north shall come against him like a whirlwind, with chariots, and with horsemen, and with many ships; and he shall enter into the countries, and shall overflow and pass over.[17]

—DANIEL 11:40

And the sixth angel poured out his vial upon the great river Euphrates; and the water thereof was dried up, that the way of the kings of the east might be prepared.[18]

—REVELATION 16:12

19 As a result, two hundred million Chinese soldiers will cross the Euphrates River and march toward Palestine.

20 With the armies of the leading world powers converging on Palestine, a showdown will be imminent. What began as a conflict between the Antichrist and the northern confederacy will escalate into an all-out war, the goal of which will be to destroy every Israelite. Anti-Semitic frenzy will grip the armies as they turn upon the Jews, many of whom will have vainly fled to desert refuges in hope of escaping the impending disaster in their land. The armies will besiege Jerusalem first and then assemble in the valley of Megiddo, a place called in Hebrew *Armageddon*, or the Mount of Slaughter. It is the last day of Daniel's seventieth week.

And the sixth angel sounded, and I heard a voice from the four horns of the golden altar which is before God, Saying to the sixth angel which had the trumpet, Loose the four angels which are bound in the great river Euphrates. And the four angels were loosed, which were prepared for an hour, and a day, and a month, and a year, for to slay the third part of men. And the number of the army of the horsemen *were* two hundred thousand thousand: and I heard the number of them.[19]

—Revelation 9:13–16

Armageddon

And I saw three unclean spirits like frogs *come* out of the mouth of the dragon, and out of the mouth of the beast, and out of the mouth of the false prophet. For they are the spirits of devils, working miracles, *which* go forth unto the kings of the earth and of the whole world, to gather them to the battle of that great day of God Almighty. Behold, I come as a thief. Blessed *is* he that watcheth, and keepeth his garments, lest he walk naked, and they see his shame. And he gathered them together into a place called in the Hebrew tongue Armageddon. And the seventh angel poured out his vial into the air; and there came a great voice out of the temple of heaven, from the throne, saying, It is done. And there were voices, and thunders, and lightnings; and there was a great earthquake, such as was not since men were upon the earth, so mighty an earthquake, *and* so great. And the great city was divided into three parts, and the cities of the nations fell: and great Babylon came in remembrance before God, to give unto her the cup of the wine of the fierceness of his wrath. And every island fled away, and the mountains were not found. And there fell upon men a great hail out of heaven, *every stone* about the weight of a talent: and men blasphemed God because of the plague of the hail; for the plague thereof was exceeding great.[20]

—Revelation 16:13–21

21 At the very moment when it seems God's chosen people will be destroyed, Jesus, the son of David, will suddenly appear in the sky to execute vengeance upon the Antichrist and his armies and allies. Mounted on a white horse, he will be called "Faithful and True," and with justice he will judge and make war. His eyes will be like blazing fire, and on his head he will wear many crowns. He will be dressed in a robe dipped in blood, and his name will be The Word of God. On his robe and thigh will be written "KING OF KINGS, AND LORD OF LORDS." The armies of heaven, his saints, will follow behind him riding on white horses and dressed in fine linen, clean and white. A sharp sword will come out of the mouth of the Lord, and in one fell swoop he will strike down the nations and thereafter rule over them with an iron scepter. He will deliver the Jewish remnant that the Gentile world powers, led by the beast and false prophet, had besieged. The beast and false prophet will be summarily cast into the lake of fire.

Thus, the battle of Armageddon will end in the greatest slaughter in the history of humankind. So many people will be killed that the pool of blood in the valley will reach to the horses' bridles. Seven months of sustained labor will be required to bury the dead. The birds and wild animals will have an enormous feast, for they will "eat the flesh of the mighty, and drink the blood of the princes of the earth, of rams, of lambs, and of goats, of bullocks, all of them fatlings of Bashan" (Eze. 39:18).

And I saw heaven opened, and behold a white horse: and he that sat upon him *was* called Faithful and True, and in righteousness he doth judge and make war. His eyes *were* as a flame of fire, and on his head *were* many crowns; and he had a name written, that no man knew, but he himself. And he *was* clothed with a vesture dipped in blood: and his name is called The Word of God. And the armies *which were* in heaven followed him upon white horses, clothed in fine linen, white and clean. And out of his mouth goeth a sharp sword, that with it he should smite the nations: and he shall rule them with a rod of iron: and he treadeth the winepress of the fierceness and wrath of Almighty God. And he hath on *his* vesture and on his thigh a name written, KING OF KINGS, AND LORD OF LORDS.... And I saw the beast, and the kings of the earth, and their armies, gathered together to make war against him that sat on the horse, and against his army. And the beast was taken, and with him the false prophet that wrought miracles before him, with which he deceived them that had received the mark of the beast, and them that worshipped his image. These both were cast alive into a lake of fire burning with brimstone. And the remnant were slain with the sword of him that sat upon the horse, which *sword* proceeded out of his mouth: and all the fowls were filled with their flesh.[21]

—REVELATION 19:11–16, 19–21

22 After the Battle of Armageddon, Jesus shall stand on the Mount of Olives and take possession of his kingdom (Zech. 14:4). The survivors of Israel will be regathered and judged, as will the Gentile nations (Eze. 20:37–38; Matt. 25:31–46). Then the thousand-year reign of Christ—the millennium—will begin, while Satan is bound and placed in a prison called "the abyss."

23 Israel will possess the promised land in perpetuity, fulfilling God's covenant with Abraham; Christ, a descendant of David, will occupy the Davidic throne for eternity, fulfilling God's covenant with David; and the people of Israel will receive their Messiah.

The Millennium

And I saw an angel come down from heaven, having the key of the bottomless pit and a great chain in his hand. And he laid hold on the dragon, that old serpent, which is the Devil, and Satan, and bound him a thousand years, and cast him into the bottomless pit, and shut him up, and set a seal upon him, that he should deceive the nations no more, till the thousand years should be fulfilled: and after that he must be loosed a little season. And I saw thrones, and they sat upon them, and judgment was given unto them: and I saw the souls of them that were beheaded for the witness of Jesus, and for the word of God, and which had not worshipped the beast, neither his image, neither had received his mark upon their foreheads, or in their hands; and they lived and reigned with Christ a thousand years. But the rest of the dead lived not again until the thousand years were finished. This is the first resurrection. Blessed and holy is he that hath part in the first resurrection; on such the second death hath no power, but they shall be priests of God and of Christ, and shall reign with him a thousand years.[22]

—Revelation 20:1–6

And it shall come to pass in the last days, that the mountain of the Lord's house shall be established in the top of the mountains, and shall be exalted above the hills; and all nations shall flow unto it. And many people shall go and say, Come ye, and let us go up to the mountain of the Lord, to the house of the God of Jacob; and he will teach us of his ways, and we will walk in his paths: for out of Zion shall go forth the law, and the word of the Lord from Jerusalem. And he shall judge among the nations, and shall rebuke many people: and they shall beat their swords into plowshares, and their spears into pruning hooks: nation shall not lift up sword against nation, neither shall they learn war any more.[23]

—Isaiah 2:2–4

24 Many Hebrew Bible prophecies describe the millennial kingdom as a glorious time of political justice, social harmony, material prosperity, and spiritual renewal. Nature will also share in the millennial blessings by being abundantly productive. Even ferocious beasts will be tamed and evil will be held in check by Christ who rules with "a rod of iron" (Rev. 19:15). The converted Jews will be the center of this golden age, and Christ will rule from his capital in Jerusalem. Some premillennialists have taught that during the millennium dead believers will be resurrected with their glorified bodies to mingle freely with the rest of the inhabitants of the earth.

25 At the end of the millennium, Satan will escape from captivity and lead a brief rebellion. His forces will besiege the saints, but God will send down fire from heaven to devour them. Satan will then be dispatched to the "lake of fire," where he will remain forever. This is followed by the resurrection of all the unrighteous dead. They will stand before the great white throne, where they will be judged according to their works before they are sentenced to eternal damnation.

The wolf also shall dwell with the lamb, and the leopard shall lie down with the kid; and the calf and the young lion and the fatling together; and a little child shall lead them. And the cow and the bear shall feed; their young ones shall lie down together: and the lion shall eat straw like the ox. And the sucking child shall play on the hole of the asp, and the weaned child shall put his hand on the cockatrice' den.[24]

—ISAIAH 11:6–8

The Last Judgment

And when the thousand years are expired, Satan shall be loosed out of his prison, And shall go out to deceive the nations which are in the four quarters of the earth, Gog and Magog, to gather them together to battle: the number of whom *is* as the sand of the sea. And they went up on the breadth of the earth, and compassed the camp of the saints about, and the beloved city: and fire came down from God out of heaven, and devoured them. And the devil that deceived them was cast into the lake of fire and brimstone, where the beast and the false prophet *are*, and shall be tormented day and night for ever and ever. And I saw a great white throne, and him that sat on it, from whose face the earth and the heaven fled away; and there was found no place for them. And I saw the dead, small and great, stand before God; and the books were opened: and another book was opened, which is *the book* of life: and the dead were judged out of those things which were written in the books, according to their works. And the sea gave up the dead which were in it; and death and hell delivered up the dead which were in them: and they were judged every man according to their works. And death and hell were cast into the lake of fire. This is the second death. And whosoever was not found written in the book of life was cast into the lake of fire.[25]

—REVELATION 20:7–15

26 Then the new heaven, new earth, and New Jerusalem will appear, becoming the eternal dwelling place of all those from every age who have been saved by their faith. This group of believers will include the Hebrew Bible saints, members of the church from every part of the world, Jews who were faithful to God during the tribulation and acknowledged Jesus as their Lord and Savior when he appeared, and even those born during the millennium whose hearts were genuinely obedient to Christ.

◆ The narrative of end-times events that emerges from the Bible using dispensationalist techniques is captivating and might seem to summarily preclude any scripturally based alternative understanding of the earth's final days. Indeed, the conviction that Christ will come to establish a literal kingdom on earth at some time in the future can be traced to some of Christianity's earliest leaders, many of whose teachings about the millennium dovetail nicely with modern dispensational beliefs.

Yet even in the writings of these earliest Christian teachers, we can detect crucial differences of opinion, both in what the millennium will look like and, more fundamentally, in how the Bible (and even pagan sources) should be interpreted to understand its apocalyptic passages. From the beginning there were divergent, even antagonistic, perspectives within Christian orthodoxy—a tension that to one extent or another has marked the study of the end times ever since. To see the beginnings of this controversy, we have only to turn to the writings of the Church Fathers.

And I saw a new heaven and a new earth: for the first heaven and the first earth were passed away; and there was no more sea. And I John saw the holy city, new Jerusalem, coming down from God out of heaven, prepared as a bride adorned for her husband. And I heard a great voice out of heaven saying, Behold, the tabernacle of God *is* with men. And he will dwell with them, and they shall be his people, and God himself shall be with them, *and be* their God. And God shall wipe away all tears from their eyes; and there shall be no more death, neither sorrow, nor crying, neither shall there be any more pain: for the former things are passed away. And he that sat upon the throne said, Behold, I make all things new. And he said unto me, Write: for these words are true and faithful. And he said unto me, It is done. I am Alpha and Omega, the beginning and the end. I will give unto him that is athirst of the fountain of the water of life freely.[26]

—REVELATION 21:1–6

◆ Dispensational premillennialists and many Protestants share a respect for the Church Fathers, especially those who lived before the fifth century. These early prominent Christian writers are supposed to more accurately represent the teachings of the New Testament because they lived closer to apostolic times and before Christianity was legalized by the Emperor Constantine. The post-Constantinian church is represented as less pure than in the earlier times because it was popular to be a Christian, and less sincere people adopted a diluted form of the faith.

The Church Fathers command special respect because of their orthodoxy, holiness of life, and antiquity, and many believe that the Fathers deserve serious consideration as those who have preceded us in the faith and made a serious attempt to express biblical and apostolic truth. Their support is thus valuable, their opinions demand careful study, they are to be set aside only for good reasons, and their work constitutes a challenge to us.

Dispensationalists point out that many of the Fathers were also premillennialists—they taught that the second coming of Christ would establish a millennial kingdom on earth. They readily admit that the Church Fathers do not explain Christ's second coming with all the details of later writers, but their literal approach to the second coming is a great encouragement to dispensationalists and demonstrates that from the very beginning Christians have speculated about the nature of the end times.

1 Papias is one of the first individuals who clearly taught millenarianism in the early church. His teaching, like that of the book of Revelation, goes back to Jewish apocalyptic sources. Papias is believed to have been bishop of Hierapolis in Phrygia sometime during the first half of the second century and to have suffered martyrdom. He had personal contact with the disciples of Jesus, especially John. We have some of his work preserved by Irenaeus and Eusebius, and in these fragments Papias states his belief in a peaceful, abundant, and harmonious millennium quite clearly. "There will be a millennium after the resurrection from the dead, when the personal reign of Christ will be established on this earth," he writes, and goes on to describe the details of his vision.

2 □ Premillennialism and the Church Fathers

Papias

from *Fragments of Papias*

The days will come in which vines shall grow, having each ten thousand branches, and in each branch ten thousand twigs, and in each true twig ten thousand shoots, and in every one of the shoots ten thousand clusters, and on every one of the clusters ten thousand grapes, and every grape when pressed will give five-and-twenty metretes of wine. And when any one of the saints shall lay hold of a cluster, another shall cry out, 'I am a better cluster, take me; bless the Lord though me,' In like manner, [he said] that a grain of wheat would produce ten thousand ears, and that every ear would have ten thousand grains, and every grain would yield ten pounds of clear, pure, fine flour; and that apples, and seeds, and grass would produce in similar proportions; and that all animals, feeding them only on the productions of the earth, would become peaceable and harmonious, and be in perfect subjection to man.[1]

◆ Another believer in the millennium, Irenaeus was bishop of Lyon at the end of the second century, having been born in Asia Minor about the year 130. Although he was educated in the East, he became one of the most renowned of the Western Fathers. Irenaeus claimed that in his youth he had been taught by Polycarp, who had had personal acquaintance with the apostle John.

Irenaeus exemplifies the still-common approach of filling in the predictions of the book of Revelation with details from the Hebrew scriptures in order to make the picture of the end times more vivid and concrete. He viewed the millennial reign as an age of paradise on earth, when the just would rise again and rule the world. The righteous would receive their rewards at the time of this kingdom for all that they had given up for Christ and for what they had given to the poor. The time of the millennium was also to be a conditioning of the righteous to behold the glory of the Father for all eternity.

2 For Irenaeus, the millennium is the redemption of the children of God referred to by Paul in Romans 8:19. The center of this reign will be Jerusalem, and it is there that the affairs of the earth will be managed by the Lord as his capital city on earth. Irenaeus refuted the allegorical interpretation of prophecies, which he felt were to be applied literally to the earth after the time of the Antichrist and the resurrection of the just.

Irenaeus

from *Against the Heretics*

If, however, any shall endeavor to allegorize [prophecies] of this kind, they shall not be found consistent with themselves on all points, and shall be confuted by the teaching of the very expression [in question]. For example: 'When the cities' of the Gentiles 'shall be desolate, so that they be not inhabited, and the houses so that there shall be no men in them, and the land shall be left desolate.' 'For, behold,' says Isaiah, 'the day of the Lord cometh past remedy, full of fury and wrath, to lay waste the city of the earth, and to root sinners out of it.' And again he says, 'Let him be taken away, that he behold not the glory of God.' And when these things are done, he says, 'God will remove men far away, and those that are left shall multiply in the earth.' 'And they shall build houses, and shall inhabit them themselves: and plant vineyards, and eat of them themselves.' For all these and other words were unquestionably spoken in reference to the resurrection of the just, which takes place after the coming of Antichrist, and the destruction of all nations under his rule; in [the times of] which [resurrection] the righteous shall reign in the earth, waxing stronger by the sight of the Lord.[2]

◆ Another early Father of the Church who held millenarian views was Justin Martyr, the earliest Christian apologist. Justin was born in Samaria in 100 C.E. and received a liberal Hellenic education, which inspired in him a thirst for truth. Justin was converted by the witness of a layman who stressed the fulfillment of the Hebrew scripture prophecies concerning the incarnation of Christ. He then devoted his life to a defense of the faith at a time when profession of Christianity was a crime under Roman law. He finally sealed his testimony with his blood; so he earned his name Martyr.

3 His dialogue with Trypho, the most distinguished Jew of his day, is assumed to be a free rendering of a disputation that actually occurred as Justin tried to win Trypho to the Christian faith. In the course of this disputation Trypho asks whether Justin really believes in a second coming of Christ to establish the millennium and to raise the saints to a life of bliss here on earth. To prove the truth of his teaching, Justin appeals to Isaiah, the Gospels, and the book of Revelation (sometimes known as the Apocalypse of John).

4 Another famous Church Father, Tertullian, also defended the millennial hope. Born at Carthage in 160 C.E., Tertullian received a Greco-Roman education and became a lawyer. Converted to Christianity, he became one of the most outspoken defenders that the faith has ever produced. Tertullian claimed that the Christians have a millennial hope for this world. He also claimed that the soldiers of the Roman army had seen the New Jerusalem—"a picture of this very city"—hovering in the morning sky in Palestine for forty days.

Justin Martyr

from *Dialogue with Trypho, a Jew*

And further, there was a certain man with us, whose name was John, one of the apostles of Christ, who prophesied, by a revelation that was made to him, that those who believed in our Christ would dwell a thousand years in Jerusalem; and that thereafter the general, and, in short, the eternal resurrection and judgment of all men would likewise take place. Just as our Lord also said, 'They shall neither marry nor be given in marriage, but shall be equal to the angels, the children of the God of the resurrection.'[3]

Tertullian

from *The Five Books of Quintus Sept. Flor.*

But we do confess that a kingdom is promised to us upon the earth, although before heaven, only in another state of existence; inasmuch as it will be after the resurrection for a thousand years in the divinely-built city of Jerusalem, 'let down from heaven' which the apostle also calls 'our mother from above'; and, while declaring that our ... citizenship, is in heaven, he predicated of it that it is really a city in heaven. This both Ezekiel had knowledge of, and the Apostle John beheld. And the word of the new prophecy which is a part of our belief, attests how it foretold that there would be for a sign a picture of this very city exhibited to view previous to its manifestation.[4]

5 Hippolytus (d. 236), bishop of Portus Romanus, was another capable third-century advocate of millenarianism. The city of which he was bishop was located on a harbor some fifteen miles from Rome on the northern side of the mouth of the Tiber. He was a renowned theologian holding to a future advent of Christ at the time of the resurrection of the saints. To calculate the timing of this event, he assumed that Genesis's six days of creation and seventh day of rest each represented 1,000 years of human history. Hence, 6,000 years after creation, the time would come for the Sabbath rest of 1,000 years—in other words, the millennium. As his justification for this interpretation, he appealed to the book of Psalms, which says that a day with the Lord is as a thousand years. Using typology—where certain numbers and events in the Hebrew scriptures are supposed to represent, or be "types" of, other realities—Hippolytus set the date of Christ's birth in the year 5500 (from the time of creation), yielding a date for Christ's return at the year 500 C.E. So from Hippolytus' time to the second coming of Christ would be about 250 years according to his calculations. The urge to set a specific date for Christ's return is almost as old as the Christian church itself.

Hippolytus

from *On Daniel*

But some one may be ready to say, How will you prove to me that the Saviour was born in the year 5500? Learn that easily, O man; for the things that took place of old in the wilderness, under Moses, in the case of the tabernacle, were constituted types and emblems of spiritual mysteries, in order that, when the truth came in Christ in these last days, you might be able to perceive that these things were fulfilled. For He says to him, 'And thou shalt make the ark of imperishable wood and shalt overlay it with pure gold within and without, and thou shalt make the length of it two cubits and a half, and the breadth thereof one cubit and a half, and a cubit and a half the height'; which measures, when summed up together, make five cubits and a half, so that the 5500 years might be signified thereby.[5]

◆　Although the doctrine of the millennium tended to die out in the Greek-speaking or Eastern Church, it continued for a longer period in the West through the writing and preaching of individuals such as Commodianus. A Christian Latin poet of the mid-third century, Commodianus was an early Church Father who set forth one of the more detailed millennialist systems. He identified numerous signs that would precede the Antichrist and showed that the Man of Sin was predicted in Isaiah. He also spelled out in detail the Antichrist's reign and military campaigns.

6　Commodianus followed Hippolytus's millennial Sabbath theory and argued that those who have been devoted to Christ, the martyrs, will experience the first resurrection. They will rise again and become incorruptible. All the good things of the earth will be at the martyrs' disposal. They shall receive the blessings that had been denied to them because of their sacrificial deaths, such as marriage and offspring. Universal peace will prevail, the earth's climate will be ideal, and the land will bear fruit in abundance. Certain classes of sinners, especially those who were higher on the racial and social scale, shall provide the saints with servants during the thousand-year reign. These sinners will be given a chance to repent, but Commodianus was not specific on this matter. After the millennium will come the final judgment.

Commodianus

from *The Instructions of Commodianus in Favour of Christian Discipline, Against the God of the Heathens*

I add something, on account of unbelievers, of the Day of Judgment. Again, the fire of the Lord sent forth shall be appointed. The earth gives a true groan ... and the whole of nature is converted in flame, which yet avoids the camp of His saints. The earth is burned up from its foundations, and the mountains melt. Of the sea nothing remains: it is overcome by the powerful fire. This sky perishes, and the stars and these things are changed. Another novelty of sky and of everlasting earth is arranged. Thence they who deserve it are sent away in a second death, but the righteous are placed in inner dwelling-places.[6]

7 | The last early premillenarian with which we will deal is Lactantius, who was born in 250 C.E. in Africa and was converted to Christianity as an adult. He was so well trained in rhetoric that he earned the name "Christian Cicero." He lived during the last of the great Roman persecutions and the legalization of Christianity under Constantine. Then he became the tutor of the emperor's son, Crispus. His most famous work, *The Divine Institutes*, is the first attempt at a systematic Christian theology. In this book he describes the millennium, but, surprisingly, he adds to the customary biblical material of the Hebrew prophets and the book of Revelation details from the Sibylline Oracles (religious utterances made by prophetesses in pagan Rome). His statement about the millennium is one of the most lucid of the early Fathers.

◆ | When Constantine legalized Christianity in the fourth century, much of the need for millennial teaching was alleviated. A new eschatology was developed from the earlier work of a number of scholars, one of these being Origen (185–254), the precocious neo-Platonic mystic of Alexandria. He represented a more complicated interpretation of scripture. He believed that the Bible was a living organism consisting of three parts: a literal sense, furnished by the meaning of the words; a moral sense for general edification; and a mystic sense, for those who are able to attain the high ground of philosophical speculation.

Lactantius

from *The Divine Institutes*

Then they who shall be alive in their bodies shall not die, but during those thousand years shall produce an infinite multitude, and their offspring shall be holy, and beloved by God; but they who shall be raised from the dead shall preside over the living as judges. But the nations shall not be entirely extinguished, but some shall be left as a victory for God, that they may be the occasion of triumph to the righteous, and may be subjected to perpetual slavery. About the same time also the prince of the devils, who is the contriver of all evils, shall be bound with chains, and shall be imprisoned during the thousand years of the heavenly rule in which righteousness shall reign in the world, so that he may contrive no evil against the people of God. After His coming the righteous shall be collected from all the earth, and the judgment being completed, the sacred city shall be planted in the middle of the earth, in which God Himself the builder may dwell together with the righteous, bearing rule in it. And the Sibyl marks out this city when she says: 'And the city which God made, this He made more brilliant than the stars, and sun, and moon.' Then that darkness will be taken away from the world with which the heaven will be overspread and darkened, and the moon will receive the brightness of the sun, nor will it be further diminished: but the sun will become seven times brighter than it now is; and the earth will open its fruitfulness, and bring forth most abundant fruits of its own accord; the rocky mountains shall drop with honey; streams of wine shall run down, and rivers flow with milk: in short, the world itself shall rejoice, and all nature exult, being rescued and set free from the dominion of evil and impiety, and guilt and error. Throughout this time, beasts shall not be nourished by blood, nor birds by prey; but all things shall be peaceful and tranquil. Lions and calves shall stand together at the manger, the wolf shall not carry off the sheep, the hound shall not hunt for prey; hawks and eagles shall not injure; the infant shall play with serpents. In short, those things shall then come to pass which the Poets spoke of as being done in the reign of Saturnus.[7]

8   Origen denounced premillennialists as visionaries, deluded fools, and
slavish literalists. He characterized them as those who looked for the
rebuilding of Jerusalem with gold and precious stones, expecting that
the heathen would be their slaves, and that they would receive the
material abundance of all the world.

   The true Christian, according to Origen, was the person of the spirit
who had no such worldly expectation. The whole hope of the Christian
is a hope of heaven; the earth is not worthy of the Christian's hope.
Origen helped to set the stage of the triumph of a more spiritualized
interpretation of the reign of Christ.

Origen

from *De Principiis*

Certain persons, then, refusing the labour of thinking, and adopting a superficial view of the letter of the law, and yielding rather in some measure to the indulgence of their own desires and lusts, being disciples of the letter alone, are of opinion that the fulfillment of the promises of the future are to be looked for in bodily pleasure and luxury; and therefore they especially desire to have again, after the resurrection, such bodily structures as may never be without the power of eating, and drinking, and performing all the functions of flesh and blood, not following the opinion of the Apostle Paul regarding the resurrection of a spiritual body. And consequently they say, that after the resurrection there will be marriages, and the begetting of children, imagining to themselves that the earthly city of Jerusalem is to be rebuilt, its foundations laid in precious stones, and its walls constructed of jasper, and its battlements of crystal; that it is to have a wall composed of many precious stones, as jasper, and sapphire, and chalcedony, and emerald, and sardonyx, and onyx, and chrystolite, and chrysoprase, and jacinth, and amethyst. Moreover, they think that the natives of other countries are to be given them as the ministers of their pleasures, whom they are to employ either as tillers of the field or builders of walls, and by whom their ruined and fallen city is again to be raised up; and they think that they are to receive the wealth of the nations to live on, and that they have control over their riches; that even the camels of Midian and Kedar will come, and bring to them gold, and incense, and precious stones.[8] And these views they think to establish on the authority of the prophets by those promises which are written regarding Jerusalem; and by those passages also where it is said, that they who serve the Lord shall eat and drink, but that sinners shall hunger and thirst; that the righteous shall be joyful, but that sorrow shall possess the wicked....

(*continued on page 41*)

◆ The great appeal of premillennialism was that it met the spiritual needs of Christians who lived under the constant threat of persecution. Its promise of an earthly millennial kingdom and emphasis on the connection between the Antichrist and the Roman Empire were clear and memorable images that were easily understandable. Chiliasm (belief in millennialism) was popular religion at its best, and it nourished the spirits of Christians during times of danger and strengthened their wills to persist in the faith.

However, in addition to these orthodox millennialists, there were some early heretical movements, such as the Montanists and the followers of Cerinthus, which also taught the reign of Christ on earth. Their teachings were often rooted in a morbid exaggeration of Christian demands and fanatical asceticism. Central to all this rigor was the teaching that every sacrifice would be rewarded when Jesus Christ would erect his earthly kingdom in Jerusalem and a good time would be had by all, complete with all the satisfactions of sensual pleasure of a nuptial feast.

These teachings tended to discredit the doctrine of the millennium in the larger Christian movement. By the end of the second century, premillennialism, already under assault from Origen, was forced to struggle under the added stigma of fanaticism and sensualism.

Moreover, other forces were at work in the third century that were undermining faith in millennialism. The crucial development was the accession of Constantine (c. 275–337) to the imperial throne. Although the degree of his Christian commitment is a matter of considerable historical debate, his edict in 313 allowing toleration of the church and his other actions favoring Christians placed them in a new relationship to the Roman state.

The millennial hope had thrived while people were under the pressure of persecution, but now in the newly "Christianized" Roman world, official hostility was past and there was a lessened need for such end-time teaching. The time was ripe for a new eschatology to replace chiliasm. Its chief pioneer lived in North Africa.

Then, again, ... they think they are to be kings and princes, like those earthly monarchs who now exist; chiefly, as it appears, on account of that expression in the Gospel: 'Have thou power over five cities.' And to speak shortly, according to the manner of things in this life in all similar matters, do they desire the fulfillment of all things looked for in the promises, viz. that what now is should exist again. Such are the views of those who, while believing in Christ, ... [draw] from them nothing worthy of the divine promises.

◆ The early premillennial view of the Church Fathers fell out of currency due to a number of influences, including the new interpretive methods of Origen, the association of millennialism with heretical movements, the legalization of Christianity by Constantine, and the amillennial teaching of the greatest of the Latin Fathers, Augustine of Hippo (354–430), truly a landmark figure in the history of Christianity. A North African, educated in the rhetorical tradition of ancient Rome, his restless energy produced a vast output, including 113 books, at least 218 letters, and more than 500 sermons. One of his most famous works is *The City of God,* on which he labored for fourteen years (412–26).

The importance of Augustine's teachings, including those on the end times, can hardly be overemphasized. Not only was the Christian philosophy of the early Middle Ages almost wholly Augustinian, but also the scholastics of the later Middle Ages and the Protestants of the Reformation base their systems upon his thought, and even modern theologians, both Catholic and Protestant, turn to his wisdom. Contemporary secular thought owes much to principles and attitudes that are Augustinian in origin.

Augustine changed the course of interpretation of the millennium in *The City of God,* where he adopted a symbolical-mystical interpretive strategy pioneered by a North African contemporary, a lay theologian and Bible commentator named Tyconius. Although Augustine believed in an actual resurrection and judgment at the end of time, he had no patience for those who speculated about Christ returning to establish a utopian reign on earth, and even less tolerance for the literalistic manner of reading the Bible that gave rise to such beliefs. This amillennial approach is evident in the following passages.

1 Revelation speaks of a "first resurrection" and a "second resurrection" of the saints. In Augustine's symbolical-mystical interpretation, the first resurrection is not a rapture-like event initiating a global Apocalypse, but is rather the change an individual Christian undergoes from the death of sin to a life of righteousness. Those millennialists who teach that the first resurrection is a literal, bodily resurrection heralding an earthly millennium, according to Augustine, are wrong. His contempt for such misinterpretations is evident.

3 □ Augustine's Spiritualized Amillennialism

from *The City of God*

Chapter 7

WHAT IS WRITTEN IN THE REVELATION OF JOHN
REGARDING THE TWO RESURRECTIONS, AND THE
THOUSAND YEARS, AND WHAT MAY REASONABLY BE HELD
ON THESE POINTS.

The evangelist John has spoken of these two resurrections in the book which is called the Apocalypse, but in such a way that some Christians do not understand the first of the two, and so construe the passage into ridiculous fancies.[1] For the Apostle John says in the foresaid book, "And I saw an angel come down from heaven.... Blessed and holy is he that hath part in the first resurrection: on such the second death hath no power; but they shall be priests of God and of Christ, and shall reign with Him a thousand years" (Rev. 20:1–6). Those, who on the strength of this passage, have suspected that the first resurrection is future and bodily, have been moved, among other things, specially by the number of a thousand years, as if it were a fit thing that the saints should thus enjoy a kind of Sabbath-rest during that period, a holy leisure after the labors of the six thousand years since man was created, and was on account of his great sin dismissed from the blessedness of paradise into the woes of this mortal life, so that thus, as it is written, "One day is with the Lord as a thousand years, and a thousand years as one day" (2 Pet. 3:8), there should follow on the completion of six thousand years, as of

(continued on page 45)

2 Augustine outlines the classic premillennialist understanding of the universal week; that is, that the six days of creation and seventh day of rest as described in Genesis symbolize six thousand years of history followed by a thousand-year "day" of rest for the faithful. He is laying the groundwork to rebuff this view.

3 Augustine admitted that at one time he had been a millennialist, but the immoderate, self-serving, carnal extremism of some of its advocates had turned him against it.

4 In Augustine's spiritual view, the binding of Satan (Rev. 20:2) is not a one-time event connected with the Apocalypse, but is rather an ongoing process that began when the church carried the gospel message beyond Judea into the other nations of the world. This fulfilled the statement of Jesus: "No man can enter into a strong man's house, and spoil his goods, except he will first bind the strong man" (Mark 3:27). The strong man is Satan, and this tying up of the Evil One is repeated whenever people are won to the Christian faith.

5 The millennium refers to the present age when, with divine help, the saints are not overcome by sin.

6 Augustine spiritualized the millennium—hence he denied that there would be a literal reign of Christ on earth at some point in the future. Christians already reign with God in God's kingdom, in the here-and-now "city of God." The millennial rule of the church will last until the end of the age, when there will be a second, literal, resurrection. The figure 1,000 indicates that this is not the future rule of eternity but the perfect rule of the church age, which will persist until the end of time.

six days, a kind of seventh-day Sabbath in the succeeding thousand years; and that it is for this purpose the saints rise, viz., to celebrate this Sabbath.[2] And this opinion would not be objectionable, if it were believed that the joys of the saints in that Sabbath shall be spiritual, and consequent on the presence of God; for I myself, too, once held this opinion. But, as they assert that those who then rise again shall enjoy the leisure of immoderate carnal banquets, furnished with an amount of meat and drink such as not only to shock the feeling of the temperate, but even to surpass the measure of credulity itself, such assertions can be believed only by the carnal.[3] They who do believe then are called by the spiritual Chiliasts, which we may literally reproduce by the name Millenarians.

Chapter 9

WHAT THE REIGN OF THE SAINTS WITH CHRIST FOR A THOUSAND YEARS IS, AND HOW IT DIFFERS FROM THE ETERNAL KINGDOM.

But while the devil is bound,[4] the saints reign with Christ during the same thousand years, understood in the same way, that is, of the time of His first coming. (Between His first and second coming.)[5] For, leaving out of account that kingdom concerning which He shall say in the end, "Come, ye blessed of my Father, take possession of the kingdom prepared for you" (Matt. 25:34), the Church could not now be called His kingdom or the kingdom of heaven unless His saints were even now reigning with Him, though in another and far different way; for to His saints He says, "Lo, I am with you always, even to the end of the world" (Matt. 28:20)....[6] Therefore the Church even now is the kingdom of Christ, and the kingdom of heaven. Accordingly, even now His saints reign with Him, though otherwise than as they shall reign hereafter....

(continued on page 47)

7 However, during the present age, the "city of God" exists alongside the "city of man" ("the beast," in scriptural terms)—that is, the world. There are two distinct societies of people; one will reign eternally with God, and the other will suffer eternal punishment. The city of God is the church, and its citizens are repentant and forgiven sinners. Whenever grace enters the hearts of people, they become citizens of the heavenly city. The citizens of the earthly city, on the other hand, are destined to never-ending punishment with the devil. The "beast [rising] up out of the sea" (Rev. 13:1) is this godless city—not a single Antichrist that could be identified as one man.

8 The "tares" refers to a parable found in Matthew 13:24–30 in which Jesus describes the kingdom of heaven: A man planted wheat in a field, but that night his enemy came and sowed weeds ("tares") among the wheat. The man's servants asked permission to pull out the weeds, but the man feared that in doing so, they would also inadvertently destroy the wheat. Therefore he counseled them to wait, declaring that "in the time of the harvest I will say to the reapers, 'Gather ye together first the tares, and bind them in bundles to burn them: but gather the wheat into my barn.'" This imagery fits well with Augustine's assertion that the city of God (the wheat) coexists with the city of man (the tares)—and also highlights what the fate of each will be "in the time of the harvest."

9 The thousand years designates the indeterminate period of time from the first coming of Christ to the end of the world, when he shall come the second time.

As to the words following, "And if any have not worshipped the beast nor his image, nor have received his inscription on their forehead, or on their hand," we must take them of both the living and the dead. And what this beast is, though it requires a more careful investigation, yet it is not inconsistent with the true faith to understand it of the ungodly city itself, and the community of unbelievers set in opposition to the faithful people and the city of God.[7] "His image" seems to me to mean his simulation, to wit, in those men who profess to believe, but live as unbelievers. For they pretend to be what they are not, and are called Christians, not from a true likeness, but from a deceitful image. For to this beast belong not only the avowed enemies of the name of Christ and His most glorious city, but also the tares[8] which are to be gathered out of His kingdom, the Church, in the end of the world.... They, then, who are free from these pollutions, whether they still live in this mortal flesh, or are dead, reign with Christ even now, through this whole interval which is indicted by the thousand years, in a fashion suited to this time.[9]

[10] Augustine again refutes narrow logic and simplistic, one-dimensional interpretations of scripture.

[11] Like the millennialists he refutes, Augustine appeals to the Bible to bolster his symbolic, spiritual interpretation, namely, that souls as well as bodies can "fall."

Chapter 10

WHAT IS TO BE REPLIED TO THOSE WHO THINK THAT
RESURRECTION PERTAINS ONLY TO BODIES AND NOT TO
SOULS.

There are some who suppose that resurrection can be predicated only of
the body, and therefore they contend that this first resurrection (of the
Apocalypse) is a bodily resurrection. For, say they, "to rise again" can
only be said of things that fall. Now, bodies fall in death. There cannot,
therefore, be a resurrection of souls, but of bodies. But what do they
say to the apostle who speaks of a resurrection of souls?[10] For certainly
it was in the inner and not the outer man that those had risen again to
whom he says, "If ye have risen with Christ, mind the things that are
above" (Col. 3:1).... As to what they say about nothing being able to rise
again but what falls, whence they conclude that resurrection pertains
to bodies only, and not to souls, because bodies fall, why do they make
nothing of the words, "Ye that fear the Lord, wait for His mercy; and
go not aside lest ye fall (Eccl[esiasticus] 2:7.); and "To his own Master he
stands or falls" (Rom. 14:4); and "He that thinketh he standeth, let him
take heed lest he fall" (I Cor. 10:12)?[11] For I fancy this fall that we are
to take heed against is a fall of the soul, not of the body. If, then, rising
again belongs to things that fall, and souls fall, it must be owned that
souls also rise again.

12 Augustine points out the absurdity of reading this portion of scripture literally. How big would such a book have to be?

13 Nevertheless, the judgment of God is real: At the very end of time, the dead will be raised, all will be judged, and the unrighteous will be consigned to everlasting torment. The teachings of scripture, even when interpreted symbolically, are not to be taken lightly.

Chapter 14

OF THE DAMNATION OF THE DEVIL AND HIS ADHERENTS;
AND A SKETCH OF THE BODILY RESURRECTION OF ALL THE
DEAD, AND OF THE FINAL RETRIBUTIVE JUDGMENT.

[John, describing his vision of the last judgment, wrote,] "And I saw the dead, great and small: and the books were opened; and another book was opened, which is the book of the life of each man: and the dead were judged out of those things which were written in the books according to their deeds."... If this book be materially considered, who can reckon its size or length, or the time it would take to read a book in which the whole life of every man is recorded?[12] Shall there be present as many angels as men, and shall each man hear his life recited by the angel assigned to him? In that case there will be not one book containing all the lives, but a separate book for every life. But our passage requires us to think of one only. "And another book was opened," it says. We must therefore understand it of a certain divine power, by which it shall be brought about that everyone shall recall to memory all his own works, whether good or evil, and shall mentally survey them with a marvelous rapidity, so that this knowledge will either accuse or excuse conscience, and thus all and each shall be simultaneously judged. And this divine power is called a book, because in it we shall as it were read all that it causes us to remember.[13]

14 Augustine now turns his attention from the judgment of the wicked to the fate of the saints, which accompanies the world being consumed by a destroying but refining fire.

15 After the final judgment, God will wipe away the tears from their eyes, and there will be no more death, grief, or sorrow. This is the "second resurrection," which Augustine does understand literally: at this time the bodies of the city of God's inhabitants will become incorruptible and immortal.

Chapter 16

OF THE NEW HEAVEN AND THE NEW EARTH.

Having finished the prophecy of judgment, so far as the wicked are concerned, it remains that he speak also of the good.[14] "And I saw," he says, "a new heaven and a new earth: for the first heaven and the first earth have passed away; and there is no more sea." (Rev. 21:1). This will take place in the order which he has by anticipation declared in the words, "I saw One sitting on the throne, from whose face heaven and earth fled." For as soon as those who are not written in the book of life have been judged and cast into eternal fire—the nature of which fire, or its position in the world or universe, I suppose is known to no man, unless perhaps the divine Spirit reveal it to some one—then shall the figure of this world pass away in a conflagration of universal fire, as once before the world was flooded with a deluge of universal water. And by this universal conflagration the qualities of the corruptible elements which suited our corruptible bodies shall utterly perish, and our substance shall receive such qualities as shall, by a wonderful transmutation, harmonize with our immortal bodies, so that, as the world itself is renewed to some better thing, it is fitly accommodated to men, themselves renewed in their flesh to some better thing.[15]

16 Augustine believed the New Jerusalem—the city of God—was already present; nevertheless, at the last judgment, the New Jerusalem will appear with greater clarity.

17 At that time, the faithful will be given new bodies, both physical and spiritual, and they will enjoy endless happiness with God.

◆ Augustine's amillennial interpretation dominated Christian eschatological teachings for centuries and has been accepted by the major Protestant bodies and the Roman Catholic Church. Despite his overwhelming and long-lasting influence, however, various radical millennial movements periodically gained fierce, and sometimes violent, followings, particularly in the medieval and Reformation eras.

Chapter 17

OF THE ENDLESS GLORY OF THE CHURCH.

"And I saw," he says, "a great city, New Jerusalem, coming down from God out of heaven, prepared as a bride adorned for her husband. And I heard a great voice from the throne, saying, Behold, the tabernacle of God is with men, and He will dwell with them, and they shall be His people, and God Himself shall be with them. And God shall wipe away all tears from their eyes; and there shall be no more death, neither sorrow, nor crying, but neither shall there be any more pain: because the former things have passed away. And He that sat upon the throne said, Behold, I make all things new" (Rev. 21:2–5). This city is said to come down out of heaven, because the grace with which God formed it is of heaven.[16] Wherefore He says to it by Isaiah, "I am the Lord that formed thee" (Isa. 45:8). It is indeed descended from heaven from its commencement, since its citizens during the course of this world grow by the grace of God, which cometh down from above through the laver of regeneration in the Holy host sent down from heaven. But by God's final judgment, which shall be administered by His Son Jesus Christ, there shall by God's grace be manifested a glory so pervading and so new, that no vestige of what is old shall remain; for even our bodies shall pass from their old corruption and mortality to new incorruption and immortality.[17]

◆ Augustine's amillennial, spiritualized view of eschatology was amazingly influential and held the majority position in the church for the next twelve centuries. There were, however, some dissenting voices, the most significant of which was Joachim of Fiore (c. 1135–1202), a Cistercian monk in southern Italy. He treated the book of Revelation as a detailed account of history, setting a precedent for later thinkers to interpret biblical prophecies in light of events in their own times, a practice that continues unabated to this day. Later medieval figures, including some followers of Francis of Assisi—the Spiritual Franciscans—took his ideas further and transformed that spiritual age into one physically located in time, a fiercely millennial time complete with warring angelic and fiendish popes.

These strands of thought continued into the Reformation era, when some enthusiasts in the sixteenth-century evangelical movement wished to see more radical changes than the major Reformers believed wise or even possible. Commonly called Anabaptists because of their view that baptism should be administered only to believers, these groups actually lacked cohesion and constituted a number of small, divergent sects. Moreover, even though some of their leaders were highly educated, most Anabaptists belonged to the lower classes. Consequently, they were scorned and persecuted as antisocial radicals.

Finally, under the pressure of persecution, some Anabaptists gave up nonviolence and set out to establish Christ's kingdom by force. One leader, Jan Matthys, led a group to Münster in Westphalia (Germany), where his preaching was so successful that the Anabaptists gained control of the entire town in 1534, declaring it a New Jerusalem. The following accounts of the terrible events that unfolded in Münster are a unique and compelling window into the intense personal dedication with which these end-times doctrines were believed, and they have clear, unsettling echoes with some religious movements in our own day.

1 Once they had seized control of the city, the Anabaptists issued a call for the faithful to "flee from Babylon" and hasten to the New Jerusalem. A great multitude found their way to Münster before it was besieged by the bishop and his allies. (Contemporary accounts of the Münster seige are translated by Hans J. Hillerbrand.)

4 □ Radical Millennialist Movements and the Church's Response in the Medieval and Reformation Eras

Anabaptist Millennialism

Dear friends, you are to know and recognize the work God has done among us so that everyone might arise to the New Jerusalem, the city of the saints, for God wants to punish the world. Let everyone watch lest he through carelessness fall under the judgment. Jan Bokelson, the prophet of Münster, has written us with all his helpers in Christ that no one can remain free under the dragon of this world, but will suffer bodily or spiritual death. Therefore let no one neglect to come unless he wishes to tempt God.[1] There is turmoil in all the world and the prophet Jeremiah says in the 51st chapter: flee from Babylon that everyone may keep his soul, then your heart will not become discouraged on account of the call heard in the lands. I say nothing more, but command you in the name of the Lord to be obedient without delay and redeem the time. Let everyone heed and remember Lot's wife. Do not look after earthly goods, be it husband, wife or child, lest you be deceived. Let no one look after an unbelieving wife or husband, nor take them along, nor look after unbelieving children who are disobedient and are not under the rod, since they are of no profit to the congregation of the Lord.

(continued on page 59)

2 The stockpiling of supplies and weapons inside a fortified compound in the name of religious teaching bears eerie and unmistakable parallels to events near Waco, Texas, in the early 1990s.

3 The Anabaptists introduced profound changes in every aspect of life within the city, including civil government and religious observance. Neither Lutherans, nor Catholics, nor Calvinists were safe from the fanatics, and all were forced to flee, leaving the wealth of the city in the hands of the millenarians. Several nuns gave an account of the aggressive means the Anabaptists adopted to enforce their agenda.

4 Many hundreds in the city were baptized and "the ungodly" were mercilessly slaughtered. A reign of terror was established within the city and all who were suspected of a lack of sympathy with the new regime were executed. At the height of the siege, Matthys was killed and one of his young disciples Jan Bockelson (Jan van Leiden) took control. He proceeded to organize the city after the pattern of Israel with twelve elders vested with the power of life and death who were to sit in judgment twice each day.

Here are available sufficient goods for the saints. Therefore do not take anything along, except money and clothes and food for travel. Whoever has a knife, lance or rifle should take it along, Whoever does not have such should buy himself such,[2] for the Lord will redeem us through his mighty hand and through his servants, Moses and Aaron. Therefore be careful and watch for the evil one. Gather half a mile from Hasselt near the mountain cloister on 24th March around noon. Be careful in all things. Be not there before the appointed day nor later, for we will not wait for any. Let no one neglect to come. If anyone stays behind, I will be innocent of his blood. Emmanuel.

On the first Monday in Lent the agitators elected a new council, consisting of immigrants, shoemakers, tailors, furriers and other artisans....[3] The following Sunday, the first Sunday of Lent, the council informed us that we should tear down our garden house and the fence, or else it would be burned down. Some of the sisters had to leave the table—we were just eating—and go into the garden and tear them down. It was wet and cold outside and it rained and snowed heavily.... The following day several Anabaptists came to our gate between eight and nine o'clock in the morning and asked that it be opened or else they would break in. When the gate was not immediately opened, they beat vehemently against it and caused us great dismay. Since they made such great noise, our priest, Master Egbert, opened the gate. They pushed their weapons, halberds, lances and spears into the gate and thus entered forcibly. They entered our church, where they took the ornaments, first the three gilded silver chalices.... They broke whatever they could not take along. Thus they broke the relics tablet. The priest had earlier taken the holy sacrament out of the monstrance and fed two of the sisters lest the intruders crust it with their feet as they have done elsewhere.[4]

(continued on page 61)

5 Another witness describes a curious turn of events within the city as the siege dragged on. Because the number of women in the city greatly exceeded the number of men and the rules regarding the relations of the sexes were rigorous, polygamy was introduced supposedly under divine guidance. Also it was revealed that Jan van Leiden was to be king over the whole earth.

6 Yet circumstances in the New Jerusalem were becoming dire. A Münsterite taken prisoner revealed the appalling state of affairs within the city.

7 The Münsterites withstood the siege for more than a year with indescribable sufferings.

Thus Jan van Leiden—together with the bishop, the preachers and the twelve elders—proclaimed concerning the married estate that it was God's will that they should inhabit the earth. Everyone should take three or four wives, or as many as were desired. However, they should live with their wives in a divine manner. This pleased some men and not others. Husbands and wives objected that the marital estate was no longer to be kept.[5]

Jan van Leiden was the first to take a second wife in addition to the one he had married in Münster. It was said that there was still another wife in Holland. Jan van Leiden continued to take more wives until he finally had fifteen. In similar fashion all the Dutchmen, Frisians and true Anabaptists had additional wives. Indeed, they compelled their first wives to go and obtain second wives for them. The devil laughed hard about this.

Yesterday, while I was inspecting the fortifications with a commanding officer, two 'brethren', a miller and the son of a rifle-maker, were captured.[6] Both stated that the common people in the city have nothing to eat but roots, sorrel, and the like. Even this is not sufficient. In the presence of the colonel and the rest of us, the miller insisted under oath that he had scraped the white off the walls, mixed it with water, and given it to his children to drink. He also said that others have done likewise and are still doing it. Both men stated that Münster certainly did not have more than two hundred men capable of bearing arms. All others were too weak and exhausted to be of any help. Men, women and children look pale like a bleached cloth; their bodies are bloated and they have huge stomachs and legs....[7]

(continued on page 63)

8 Another witness chronicled the juxtaposition between the grim reality of the situation and "the king's" grandiose promises.

9 Finally, despite the king's prophecies and assurances, their defense collapsed and their defeat was accompanied by a horrible massacre.

10 After the city fell, Jan van Leiden and two other Anabaptist leaders were executed. The episode at Münster not only discredited the Anabaptists but it also caused people to fear millennial teaching. Indeed, those who appreciated stable government had much to fear from millenarianism when it was tied into social revolt. The Münster episode lead Winston King to remark: "The historical course of the Christian hope of a thousand-year reign of Christ on earth is a curious one. It is like an underground river, now largely hidden in the depths of the Christian consciousness, now diverted into pietistic otherworldly channels, yet frequently erupting with explosive violence into the midst of contemporary life. Perchance this very unpredictability is the reason that the established churches have looked upon it with such hostility. It poses always the threat of the dissolution of established orders of life; it is the foe of existing institutions; it is the most fundamentally revolutionary element in the Christian tradition."

The food in Münster has almost all been eaten, with the exception of 300 cows and 44 horses.[8] Twenty cows are needed to feed the people, as their number is very great. There are still some 1,300 men in the city and 6,000 women, not counting the children. Permission to leave has been given to everyone who desires to do so. Within two weeks over 200 persons left.... Twenty-five horses have already been eaten, cats are roasted on spears, and mice in pans. I spoke with Bernhard Rothmann, who said, "If God does not rescue us from our enemies, we know not what to do. Rye and barley are very scarce and will all be consumed with a month or two"....

The king prophesied that the people would be delivered from their enemies before Easter. If this were not the case, they should take and burn him on the market square before all the people.[9]

The following day they were brought, one after the other, before the judge who read the indictment.[10] The king was accused of the most serious evils and crimes. Since they were known throughout Germany, no denial was possible. He replied that he had failed against governmental authority, but not against God.... However, he admitted rebaptism as well as insurrection and lese-majesty, for which he was sentenced to death....

When the king was led as the first to the place of execution, he knelt and said, with folded hands, "Father, into thy hands do I command my spirit." Then he was tied to a stake and tortured with fiery and glowing togs and eventually killed....

After the deserved punishment had been administered to these criminal men, they were put into three iron cages so that they could be seen and recognized from afar. These cages were placed high on the steeple of St. Lamberti's Church as a perpetual memorial and to warn and terrify the restless spirits lest they attempt something similar in the future. Such was the evil ending of this tragedy.

◆ The radical Anabaptists and similar groups went against the prevailing amillennial teachings of the day. However, the reformers of the sixteenth century, while still taking an Augustinian spiritualized view of the millennium, inaugurated fundamental changes that—ironically—helped set the stage for a great renewal of premillenarian interest in the seventeenth century. For example, Martin Luther advocated a more literal approach to the scriptures, and he identified the pope with the Antichrist. Both of these attitudes helped foster a literal approach to the prophetic statements of the book of Revelation. Although Luther did not believe in a millennial reign of Christ on earth, he did feel that he lived at the end of the age. The power of the papacy, the advance of the Turks, and the general disintegration of society reinforced his conviction that he lived in the time of the Antichrist, and that meant that history was coming to an end. Another influential reformer, John Calvin, opposed millennialist doctrine while unwittingly laying the groundwork for its later resurgence.

11 Instead of stirring expectations about an earthly kingdom, Calvin seemed to be concerned with focusing the Christian hope on the appearance and revelation of the Lord for the general resurrection and last judgment, the promise of which is prefigured and sealed in Jesus's own resurrection.

12 Calvin was also against the numerical calculations that preoccupied many of his English followers, content instead to wait patiently for God's plan to unfold in its own time. In commenting on Daniel chapter 12, the passage frequently used to calculate biblical numerical predictions, he states: "In numerical calculations I am no conjurer, and those who expound this passage with too great subtlety, only trifle in their own speculations, and detract from the authority of the prophecy." Calvin never wrote a commentary on the Apocalypse.

John Calvin

from *Institutes of the Christian Religion*

FROM BOOK III, CHAPTER 25, "OF THE LAST RESURRECTION"

3. ... It is difficult to believe that after our bodies have been consumed with rottenness, they will rise again at their appointed time.... Yet the full effect appeared only in Christ, who, free from all corruption, resumed a spotless body. Then, that there may be no doubt as to our fellowship with Christ in a blessed resurrection, and that we may be contented with this pledge, Paul distinctly affirms that he sits in the heavens, and will come as a judge on the last day for the express purpose of changing our vile body, "that it may be fashioned like unto his glorious body" (Phil. 3:21).[11] For he elsewhere says that God did not raise up his Son from death to give an isolated specimen of his mighty power, but that the Spirit exerts the same efficacy in regard to them that believe; and accordingly he says, that the Spirit when he dwells in us is life, because the end for which he was given is to quicken our mortal body (Rom. 7:10, 11; Col. 3:4).... [In Christ] we behold a living image of the resurrection, so it furnishes a sure evidence to support our minds, provided we faint not, nor grow weary at the long delay, because it is not ours to measure the periods of time at our own pleasure; but to rest patiently till God in his own time renew his kingdom....[12]

(continued on page 67)

13　Calvin believed that the pope was the Antichrist, but he did not teach a millennium. In fact, he dismisses the idea as a childish superstition and states that the scriptures do not support it. He calls millennialists ignorant of divine things and "malignant perverts" who are trying to overthrow the grace of God.

14　In Calvin's understanding, the thousand years refers to the long era in which the church must struggle in the world—the "church militant"—not a blessed millennium of peace and prosperity.

15　Indeed, Calvin felt that the chiliasts' expectation of a mere thousand-year reign on earth was a poor substitute for the hope of everlasting immortality with God.

5. ... But not only did Satan stupefy the senses of mankind, so that with their bodies they buried the remembrance of the resurrection; but he also managed by various fictions so to corrupt this branch of doctrine that it at length was lost. Not to mention that even in the days of Paul he began to assail it (1 Cor. 15) shortly after the Chiliasts arose, who limited the reign of Christ to a thousand years. This fiction is too puerile to need or to deserve refutation.[13] Nor do they receive any countenance from the Apocalypse, from which it is known that they extracted a gloss for their error (Rev. 20:4), since the thousand years there mentioned refer not to the eternal blessedness of the Church, but only to the various troubles which await the Church militant in this world.[14] The whole Scripture proclaims that there will be no end either to the happiness of the elect, or the punishment of the reprobate. Moreover, in regard to all things which lie beyond our sight, and far transcend the reach of our intellect, belief must either be founded on the sure oracles of God, or altogether renounced. Those who assign only a thousand years to the children of God to enjoy the inheritance of future life, observe not how great an insult they offer to Christ and his kingdom.[15] If they are not to be clothed with immortality, then Christ himself, into whose glory they shall be transformed, has not been received into immortal glory; if their blessedness is to have an end, the kingdom of Christ, on whose solid structure it rests, is temporary. In short, they are either most ignorant of all divine things, or they maliciously aim at subverting the whole grace of God and power of Christ, which cannot have their full effect, unless sin is obliterated, death swallowed up, and eternal life fully renewed.

◆ Despite the change in attitude toward the Roman Catholic Church and a more literal approach to scripture, most of the later Reformers still took a deeply negative view of millennialism and the apocalyptic approach to the Bible. They tended to identify all who believed in a millennium with radical social revolutionaries. This sentiment was so strong that various Protestant creedal statements of the day actively *condemned* belief in the millennium.

16 *The Augsburg Confession* (1530) was written by Martin Luther and his colleagues as a summary of the evangelical faith and presented to Emperor Charles V at the Diet of Augsburg. It was the earliest of the formal creedal statements, and it became the authoritative confessional standard for the Lutheran Church. It follows the Augustinian view that Christ will return at the very end of the age, and it does not mince words with regard to Anabaptist millenarianism.

Martin Luther

from *The Augsburg Confession*

ART. 17—OF CHRIST'S RETURN TO JUDGMENT.

Also they teach that, in the consummation of the world [at the last day], Christ shall appear to judge, and shall raise up all the dead, and shall give unto the godly and elect eternal life and everlasting joys; but ungodly men and the devils shall he condemn unto endless torments.

They condemn the Anabaptists who think that to condemned men and the devils shall be an end of torments. They condemn others also, who now scatter ... opinions, that, before the resurrection of the dead, the godly shall occupy the kingdom of the world, the wicked being everywhere suppressed [the saints alone, the pious, shall have a worldly kingdom, and shall exterminate all the godless].[16]

◆ *The Belgic Confession* (1561) was one of the major creeds of the Reformed (Calvinist) Church. It was written by Dutch Reformer Guy de Bray as a statement of the Calvinists in the low countries in their struggle against the Spanish. It is adopted from an earlier confession written by Calvin for the Reformed Church of France.

17 This is a vivid vision of the last judgment, but missing are speculations about specific timelines and signs of the end. This is consonant with the Augustinian view that Christ's return will not inaugurate an earthly millennium, but will rather herald the immediate beginning of everlasting life for the faithful.

Guy de Bray

from *The Belgic Confession*

ART. 37—OF THE LAST JUDGMENT.

Finally, we believe, according to the Word of God, when the time appointed by the Lord (which is unknown to all creatures) is come, and the number of the elect complete, that our Lord Jesus Christ will come from heaven, corporally and visibly, as he ascended with great glory and majesty, to declare himself Judge of the quick and the dead, burning this old world with fire and flame to cleanse it. And then all men will personally appear before this great Judge, both men and women and children, that have been from the beginning of the world to the end thereof, being summoned by the voice of the archangel, and by the sound of the trumpet of God. For all the dead shall be raised out of the earth, and their souls joined and united with their proper bodies in which they formerly lived. As for those who shall then be living, they shall not die as the others, but be changed in the twinkling of an eye, and from corruptible become incorruptible.[17]

◆ *The Savoy Declaration* (1658) is the basic statement of faith of the English Congregational Church. Most of those who helped draft the document had attended the meeting that drafted the *Westminster Confession of Faith* (1646). Consequently, the two doctrinal statements are quite similar.

18 Identifying a single man such as the pope with the Antichrist represents a distinct move away from the spiritualized understanding of the Augustinian view, where such symbols were seen as metaphors for the force of evil in the world, not a particular person.

19 Similarly, this language of the church enjoying repose in the "latter days" reflects the resurgence of millenarianism among the seventeenth-century English Reformers. As the movement continued to gain renewed vigor and popularity among the next generation of Christian teachers and believers, it once again became tinged with elements of fanaticism, increased mysticism, and, more strongly than ever before, politics.

The English Congregational Church

from *The Savoy Declaration*

CHAP. 36—OF THE CHURCH.

IV. There is no other head of the Church but the Lord Jesus Christ; nor can the Pope of Rome in any sense be head thereof; but it [he] is that Antichrist,[18] that man of sin and son of perdition that exalteth himself in the Church against Christ, and all that is called God, whom the Lord shall destroy with the brightness of his coming.

V. As the Lord is in care and love towards his Church, hath in his infinite wise providence exercised it with great variety in all ages, for the good of them that love him, and his own glory; so, according to his promise, we expect that in the latter days, Antichrist being destroyed, the Jews called, and the adversaries of the kingdom of his dear Son broken, the churches of Christ being enlarged and edified through a free and plentiful communication of light and grace, shall enjoy in this word a more quiet, peaceable, and glorious condition than they have enjoyed.[19]

◆ The major leaders of the early Reformation such as Luther and Calvin had begun by emphasizing the pure word of scripture, but in the late sixteenth and early seventeenth centuries, in an effort to prevent new heresy, creedal statements of faith were officially enforced and threatened to supersede the authority of scripture itself. The new types of orthodoxy that emerged were challenged by Pietists such as the Methodists and also by numerous apocalyptic and millennial groups. Even otherwise orthodox writers in Central Europe and England developed new methods of interpreting scripture involving Renaissance astrology and apocalyptic studies. Perhaps the religious wars also encouraged such speculation because rather than leading to a renewal of pure, apostolic Christianity as its leaders had believed, the Reformation had resulted in political conflicts culminating in the bloody Thirty Years' War and the English Puritan Revolution.

Despite the fact that orthodox Calvinists had inherited from the sixteenth-century Reformers a deep distrust of chiliasm, and Calvin himself had condemned millennialism, it was a Reformed scholar who would play a major part in the seventeenth-century revival of belief in the earthly kingdom of Christ. This theologian, Johann Heinrich Alsted (1588–1638), was a Rhineland Calvinist and teacher renowned throughout Europe.

Alsted followed Calvin's cautious eschatology in his earlier writings, but even there one can detect an interest in future events and biblical numerics. Later in his career he embraced a completely premillennial position and defended this outlook in *Diatribe de mille annis Apocalypticis*. This work was later translated into English under the title *The Beloved City*. As the Thirty Years' War was devastating his land at that time, he felt that this indeed was the end of the age; the war seems to have helped Alsted shift his eschatological views.

1 That is, the former chapters in the book of Revelation. *The Beloved City* is a careful exposition of Revelation, chapter 20, in which the apostle John writes of the thousand years. Alsted begins by summarizing the first nineteen chapters of Revelation, identifying within the biblical text certain "estate[s] of the Church" corresponding to distinct eras in history delineated by the years 0, 606, 1517, 1625, and 1694.

5 □ Seventeenth-century Revival of Premillennialism

Johann Alsted

from *The Beloved City, or, The Saints' Reign on Earth a Thousand Years*

OF THE CONNEXION OF THIS CHAPTER WITH THE FORMER.[1]

John in his *Revelation* which he received from *God*, in the year of *Christ* 94 after the Preface, *chap*. 1 to the 9 *verse*, describes seven general Visions in this order.

The first Vision is of the seven golden Candlesticks, and of so many Starres, and it is concerning the present and future estate of the seven Churches in Asia, in the 1, 2, 3, chapters.

The second Vision is of the Book shut up, and signed with seven Seals, in the 4, 5, 6 chapters. And it is concerning the estate of the Church of the New Testament after the departure of John, to the year of Christ 606.

The third Vision is of the seven Trumpets, in the 8, 9, 10, 11 chapters, and it is concerning the state of the Church from the year of Christ 606, to the year 1517.

The fourth Vision is of the woman bringing forth a childe, and of the Dragon, of the Beast, and the Lamb, in the 12, 13, 14 chapters. And it is partly a description of the Birth of Christ, partly a recapitulation and exposition of the second and third Visions, and concerning the estate of the Church of the New Testament, from the Nativity of Christ, to the year 1517.

(continued on page 77)

2 To prove that there will be a great day of earthly blessing for the church, he elsewhere cites a number of Hebrew scripture passages (such as Isa. 2:1–4, 34:1–17, Joel 3:1–2, 9–13, and Pss. 22:27, 86:9, and 117:1). These passages, which speak of the defeat of the enemies of God, peace on earth, and the conversion of the nations, if taken literally, would all point to the future millennial reign of Christ. Among these proofs he includes Daniel 12:11–12, which he felt also showed that the millennium would begin in 1694.

3 That is, a summary of Revelation 20 follows, interpreted through the commentator's own particular interpretive scheme.

4 According to Alsted, this aspect of the end times will proceed in this fashion: God will put the dragon, Satan, into the bottomless pit for a thousand years. Since Satan is imprisoned, he cannot stir wicked men against the church of God; therefore, the church enjoys outward peace, the righteous are raised from the dead, and multitudes are converted.

The fifth Vision is of the Seven Vials, in the 15 and 16 chapters; of which the three former are poured forth from the year of Christ 1517, to the year 1625; the four following shall be poured forth from the year 1625, to the year of Christ 1694, in which the 1,000 years seem to begin.[2]

The sixth Vision is partly of the punishments, as well those which are peculiarly appointed for the Whore, and her worshippers, before the beginning of the 1,000 years, in the 17, 18, 19 chapters, as also those which shall be inflicted upon all the enemies of the Church: Partly of the future happiness of the Church here upon earth, in the 20 chapter, from the 1 verse to the 7. After the end of those years, chap. 20:7, and following verses.

The seventh Vision is of the Heavenly City, chap. 21, 22.

II. THE SUM OF THIS CHAPTER.[3]

After that the Evangelist hath related what happened to the first Beast, and the false Prophet, and their followers, (chap. 19, verse 20, 21), He tells you now what happened to the Dragon himself. For the Mystery of Iniquity being overthrown, and due punishments inflicted upon the first Beast, and the false Prophet, the Angel descends from Heaven, and being endowed with great Power, he takes order that the Dragon, that is Satan, should not anymore, by the ministry of ungodly men, stir up those accustomed troubles in the Church Militant. Wherefore there being no place left him any longer for his wanted impostures, but bound up in the bottomless pit for a thousand years, the Nations are not seduced by him, until being loosened out of prison, he again makes use of his old Engines and Strategems against the Church. Therefore for the space of those whole 1,000 years the Church shall enjoy outward peace, the Martyrs being raised from the dead, and the Nations, together with the Jews, being converted to the Faith of Christ.[4] Now after the end of these thousand years, Satan is again let loose, and the Church, by reason of the War of Gog and Magog, made sensible of more grievous

(continued on page 79)

5 At the close of the thousand years, this happy condition is ended by the war of Gog and Magog (two kingdoms mentioned by the prophet Ezekiel), during which time the church is again persecuted. After this war comes the last judgment and the final destruction of evil.

6 After his summary, Alsted presents a detailed word study of the entire chapter to support millennialism, and this philological section is followed by a logical analysis of the text. He then deals with certain objections ("Object") that he felt would arise in the mind of his readers. He begins by carefully contrasting ("Answ.") his position with the "error" of the premillennialists who had preceded him, then states that most of the objections to his teaching could be boiled down to the question of whether the church can anticipate any millennial happiness on earth before the last judgment.

7 Alsted is keen to claim a quasi-Augustine spiritualized view that the millennium will be a time for spiritual fulfillment, not carnal indulgences.

8 Here he states and then responds to the objection that the thousand years is merely symbolic of a prolonged, indeterminate length of time.

9 "Lxx" are Roman numerals equaling seventy; that is, the seventy weeks of Daniel's apocalyptic timeline.

10 Alsted concludes that the millennium is, in fact, a definite period of time in which the church will experience a "happy state."

Alsted goes on to deal with other objections, including the bodily first resurrection and the reign of the resurrected saints on earth and concludes by showing the doctrines that may be drawn from this passage. Within a short time, Alsted's book had a great influence not only on the Continent but also in England—the beginning of the premillennialist revival.

afflictions than she had suffered in former times. At length he being again thrust into the bottomless pit, together with all his forces and power, the Saints shall forever reign with Christ.[5]

A CONFUTATION OF THE OBJECTIONS.[6]

XIX Object. This Opinion little differeth from the error of the Chiliasts or Millenaries ... [Answ.] 2. The Chiliasts erred in this respect, in that they maintained an eternal life here on earth, and in the City Jerusalem. That this life should consist in the enjoyment and use of all bodily pleasures, which should last only for a thousand years. And of their opinion they made this the foundation because that in the 20 chap. of Rev. there was mention made of a thousand years. Let us hear Augustine concerning them. The Cerinthians devise also to themselves a thousand years after the Resurrection which shall be in an earthly kingdom of Christ, according to the carnal pleasures of the belly and their lust: from Whence also they are called Chiliasts.... But our opinion maintains not a thousand years of carnal pleasures, but of Spiritual joys....[7]

XXV. Object. Nowhere in Scripture is there any mention of these thousand years, but in this place only. Therefore it is very likely, That these thousand years signify merely a Great time; so that a certain number is put for an uncertain.[8] Answ. 1. Here is no consequence: It is but once mentioned in Scriptures, Therefore it must not be taken literally. For also the Lxx. Weeks of Daniel [9] are but once mentioned; and yet that number Lxx. Is literally expounded; so that it is taken for a certain, finite, and determined number. 2. This phrase, [the thousand years] is several times repeated in this place. Which repetition is not without some cause. 3. From many testimonies of Scripture a little before propounded, and expounded; from diverse Arguments recited in the first Classes, or distribution, and compared with them places of Scripture, it manifestly appears, That the happy state of the Church for these thousand years, is described in this Chapter.[10]

◆ Despite opposition, millennial ideas were espoused in England by a number of writers even before the translation of Alsted's book. The most prominent of these, Joseph Mede, was a professor of Greek at Cambridge from 1610 to 1638. One of the greatest biblical scholars the English Church has produced, he became very interested in the plight of Protestants on the Continent, who suffered during the Thirty Years' War. This interest caused him to notice Alsted's millennialism, which, when viewed in the light of the trials through which the faithful were passing, led Mede to adopt the same position. He presented these views in an outline and partial exposition of the book of Revelation, titled *The Key of the Revelation*.

Mede devised his own interpretative scenario and method of interpreting the Bible. According to him, the Apocalypse should be divided into three sections, each of these beginning with a voice from heaven as a trumpet to John. Mede felt that most of these prophecies had been fulfilled during ancient and medieval times; however, the vials of judgment written about in Revelation, chapter 16, pictured more recent events leading to the Reformation and the subsequent progressive destruction of papal power, including Martin Luther's undermining church authority over large areas of Europe and the purging of Rome's representatives by reforming monarchs such as Queen Elizabeth I. The remaining, future vials were to result in a regathering of the Jews in the Holy Land—a remarkable precursor to the dispensationalist understanding of this topic so common today—the destruction of the city of Rome, and the final destruction of the wicked.

11 This defeat of the wicked is accomplished by the intervention of Christ, who then prepares the earth for the thousand-year reign. A literal resurrection of the martyrs accompanies the setting up of this kingdom. This is one of Mede's most succinct summaries of his beliefs, but he states elsewhere that when it comes to this great mystery, it is sufficient to understand the matter in general, and one should not try to apply every detail of the prophetic scriptures. The work of Mede influenced many English writers and thinkers in the seventeenth century.

Joseph Mede

from the Compendium to *The Key of the Revelation*

[The millennium is]: The seventh Trumpet, with the whole space of 1,000 years thereto appertaining, signifying the great Day of Judgment, circumscribed within two resurrections, beginning at the judgment of Antichrist, as the morning of that day, and continuing during the space of 1,000 years granted to New Jerusalem (the Spouse of Christ) upon this Earth, till the universal resurrection and judgment of all the dead, when the wicked shall be cast into Hell to be tormented forever, and the Saints translated into Heaven, to live with Christ forever.[11]

◆ John Archer was a Puritan pastor who was suspended for his non-conformity by Archbishop Laud and went into exile in 1637. He became pastor of the English Church at Arnhem in the Netherlands. Under his leadership, the congregation became a center for chiliastic preaching, and his posthumously published book about Christ's reign on earth became a favorite of many English radicals, including the political reformers known as the Fifth Monarchists.

12 Archer conceives of Christ's millennial reign as a benevolent monarchy and expressly contrasts it with the abuses of worldly rulers, reflecting a growing incorporation of political sensibilities into religious teachings.

13 Various aspects of the Catholic Church—its practices and doctrines, the papacy, even the pope himself—have often been seen as the key to unlocking the mysteries of the Apocalypse. Archer focuses on the political and historical aspects of the papacy, not on the Catholic Church's religious teachings.

John Archer

from *The Personall Reigne of Christ upon Earth*

A third state of Christ's Kingdom [is that which] I may call Monarchical ... because in this, when [Christ] enters upon it, he will govern as earthly Monarchs have done, that is, universally over the world, (in those days known and esteemed) and in a worldly visible earthly glory, not by tyranny, oppression, and sensually, but with honor, peace, riches, and whatsoever in and of the World is not sinful; having all Nations and Kingdoms doing homage to him, as the great Monarchs of the World had....[12]

This Monarchy of Christ is to be the last in the World (as it is to last to the end of this World) and therefore it is to begin when all the four Monarchies are expired and ended (Dan. 2:34–45).... The first was the Babylonian, then in being, and expiring; the second, the Medes and Persians; the third, the Grecians, under Alexander, as a Leopard, and with wings swiftly overcoming the World; the fourth, the Romans, which was stronger and more stronger than all the former, because of the many changes that should be in it, as Ten Horns or Kingdoms rise out of it, and among them, another fearful little Horn (Dan. 7:7) ... another little Horn, most blasphemous. Now, by the Ten Horns are meant ten Kingdoms, which rose out of the Western Roman Monarchy; and by the little Horn so blasphemous, is meant the Papacy.[13]... Wherefore to find out the beginning of Christ's Kingdom we must search out how long this part of the Roman Empire, which fell into Ten Kingdoms, and the Papacy shall endure, for there end is the beginning of Christ's Kingdom.

(continued on page 85)

14 Archer demonstrates the fascination with numerics that was rejected by Calvin and the major Protestant Reformers.

15 Archer's numeric speculation yields a target date that is fast approaching—1666.

Now, how long this papacy shall last, is told Daniel, but hiddenly and sealed up so that he could not understand it, because it was about the Gentiles converted, which was a mystery not known until Christ came (Dan. 12:6, 7, 8, 9). But in the Revelation, Christ by his death purchased the privilege to open this secret (Rev. 5:4 to 11), therefore (Rev. 10:6–10), Christ comes with the Book open, whereas to Daniel it was shut ... and shows what is meant by time, times, and half a time, which in Dan. were set down in these dark words, which none could interpret ... but Christ expounded it to be 42 months, or 1260 days, a day signifying a year, thus long from the beginning of the 10 Kingdoms in Europe, and the Papacy shall prevail over the holy people and Saints of God, and then shall it be no more, and Christ will come and set up his Kingdom.[14]

I answer. Historians are diverse in account some 4 or 6 years, but about the year of our Lord and Christ 400 or 406 the Bishop of Rome began to usurp Papal power, and about that time some of the 10 Kingdoms in Europe began to arise; now let us reckon it 406 when it began, and this is the last account; then add to 406 the 1260 and it maketh 1666 which is the time made the number of the Beast (Rev. 13:18), that is, the Papacy's duration (Dan. 5:26), thy Kingdom is numbered and finished, in which number the millienary or thousand is left out, because it comes seldom, as we used to say; the Spanish Armado coming against us, was overthrown in 588 and the Papist's Powder-treason in 605 so then the end of the Papacy is to be Anno 1666....[15]

... For by the Mystery of God is meant the Kingdom of Christ, as it explained (chap. 11, 15). So that there is hope from 666 forwards, things will go well with the Protestants, or Gentile Christians, until the Thousand years begin, except one assault, which shall not hurt, but fear them, and is to usher in the coming of Christ, of which anon we will speak....

... So that it is likely, that Christ's coming from Heaven; and raising the dead, and beginning his Kingdom, and the thousand years, will be about the year of our Lord 1700, for it is to be about forty-five years after 1650 or 1656....

(continued on page 87)

16 One of the risks inherent in prophesying about specific years is that the target date may come and go without the hoped-for prophecy coming true, such as Archer's prediction here. Yet the urge to make such calculations persists throughout the history of the church. The hope for Christ's imminent return is a resilient one.

◆ The Fifth Monarchists, or Fifth Monarchy men, were active from 1649 to 1661 during the period following the Puritan Revolution. They took their name from the four monarchies of Daniel, chapter 2. This text describes a dream of Nebuchadnezzar in which four previous empires (Assyrian, Persian, Greek, and Roman) would be overthrown and the millennial reign of Christ would be established. Because the Catholic-friendly King Charles I was executed and the year 1666 was approaching, they believed that they were living at the time when King Jesus would begin to rule. They departed from Mede and Alsted in applying certain radical prophecies to contemporary events in England, and they felt that the established church should be dismantled and that the common law should be replaced by a law code based on the Bible.

The Fifth Monarchists introduced politics squarely into their religious fervor. They supported the nominated, or "Barebones," Parliament of 1653; when it collapsed and the controversial political and military leader Oliver Cromwell established his Protectorate, they condemned him and plotted against his government. Some of them were arrested and the others scattered. When the royal government under Charles II was restored, a final rebellion was crushed and the movement was discredited.

◆ After studying medicine at Cambridge University, John Rogers (1627–65) became a Presbyterian and later an Independent pastor. He joined the Fifth Monarchists and wished to have God's kingdom established by the abolition of tithes, reduction of taxes, revision of the legal system, and removal of corruption in church and state. Because Cromwell would not follow his reforming ideas, he opposed the Protectorate and was imprisoned in 1654. He continued to condemn the government as Antichrist, and his prison cell at Lambeth Palace became a center of Fifth Monarchist agitation.

Thus we have some comfort, in that there is hope the troubles on us Gentile Christians shall cease about 666.[16] But until those days, we are like to see sad times, even till Anno Domini 1666. For it is to be feared, that Popery shall again overrun Europe, and bring back under Papal power every Kingdom in Europe, and so suppress all opposers in every Kingdom by Papal power.

John Rogers

from *Fifth Monarchy Statements*

Daniel tells us of four Beasts. The last of these beasts had ten horns, amongst which rose another little horn, and this little horn persecuted the saints till the judgment sat, when they took away his dominion and destroyed it forever.

Now the four Beasts are the four great Monarchies; the ten horns are the ten European kingdoms which arose out of the last of those Monarchies. As concerning the little horn, "with much assurance and clear fight," he asserts it to be William the Conqueror and his Norman successors, all fierce persecutors of the saints, but cut off at last and forever by "the Judgment, which was Anno 1648 in that High Court of Judicature erected for the King's trial." After this comes the Fifth Monarchy. By 1660 the work of this monarchy is to get as far as Rome, and by 1666, is to be visible in all the earth. It will come mysteriously, suddenly, and terribly, and will redeem the people—1, from ecclesiastical bondage, decrees, councils, orders, and ordinances of the Pope, priest, prelate, or the like; 2, from civil bondage and slavery, or those bloody, base, unjust, accursed, tyrannical laws and sin-monopolizing lawyers as now oppress and afflict the people. And so he calls on the Parliament—the Barebones Parliament, then sitting—to prepare everything for the entry of the Fifth Monarchy; and, in order to this—1. To appoint none except the Saints to place or office. 2. To abolish all those unjust and cruel laws, and to pull down those courts,

(continued on page 89)

17 Rogers's religiously motivated demands read strikingly like a political treatise.

◆ Anna Trapnel (fl. 1642–60) was the daughter of a London shipwright. She was converted by Baptist preaching, joined the Fifth Monarchists, and became a prophet. She would fall into trances lasting as long as twelve days, and by 1654 she had become a celebrity.

18 Her visions were political, explaining the coming millennium and condemning Oliver Cromwell for his "great pomp and revenue while the poor are ready to starve."

terms, and lawyers, year, and tithes, too, which have occasioned such actions, continued complaints, and vexations to the people, and wrongs to God and men, good and bad. 3. To set up God's law alone, being that in Deut. 6:1.[17]

Anna Trapnel

from *Prophecies*

Daniels visions were very choice,
And much there lay therein,
Touching his power and his reign,
That is exalted to be King.
Daniel declares of his high seat,
And of his royal throne;
In the midst of his Captivity,
He beheld the smiting stone.
The little stone that so should smite
Upon the Image strong,
And that should have a power for
To hurl them all along.

. . . .

Spirit and Voice hath made a league
Against Cromwell and his Crown,
The which I am confident the Lord
Will ere long so strike down.[18]
Spirit and Voice hath made a league against him
That hath such a Traytor been,
And acted such false treachery
Against the mighty King.
But him the Lord will come forth against,
And his posterity
They shall not sit upon his throne,

(continued on page 91)

19 Due to her political activities Trapnel was imprisoned but was released and faded from the scene.

Trapnel is typical of several women who were active as preachers and prophets among the English civil war sects. As Robert Leach, a prominent Quaker, explains: "Because everyone is illumined by the Holy Spirit, the spoken ministry is, of course, not limited to men. All Friends, men or women, are welcome to stand up and speak.... They were not unique in this position. Baptists and others had women preachers. The scornful designation of 'she-preachers' was given to them in a list of errors, heresies, and blasphemies in a seventeenth-century anti-Baptist tract. 'An audacious virago' is an expression used elsewhere."

That he hath lifted up so high.
The Voice and Spirit hath made a league
Against Church-members all,
Who fall in with apostates, and
Endeavour to build up their wall;

. . . .

England did promise and engage
Great things for God to do:
But now, alas, they are started from
His interest so true.
Cromwell he did appear for Christ,
And did much blood engage
For him, and for his interest,
His enemies to enslave.
When Cromwell came forth in his name,
Victory did abound;
For he did say he came for Christ,
And to exalt his Crown.
He fetcht his government from Christ,
O 'twas a master-sin.[19]

◆ Daniel Whitby (1638–1726) is considered by many to be the one who systematized postmillennialism, a movement that, like premillennialism, also posited an extended millennial period of peace on earth for the church (and all humankind), but one that would be reached gradually through the efforts of humanity and the workings of the Holy Spirit, not one ushered in suddenly by cataclysmic events and Christ's sudden return.

Whitby was rector of St. Edmund's Church, Salisbury. He held that the earth's population would be converted to Christ, the Jews restored to the Holy Land, and the pope and Turks vanquished, and then the world would enjoy a thousand-year golden age of universal peace, happiness, and righteousness. At the close of this period, Christ would personally come to earth and the last judgment would take place. Whitby's more optimistic outlook continued to be influential as his writings were reprinted into the mid-nineteenth century.

1 For Whitby, no rapture of the living or the dead would accompany the beginning of the millennium.

2 The history of eschatological interpretation shows an increasing interest in the role of Jews and the nation of Israel in the pattern of end-times events.

3 Though their differences are significant, the postmillennial and premillennial views have a number of beliefs in common.

6 □ Eighteenth-century Postmillennialism

Daniel Whitby

from A Paraphrase and Commentary on the New Testament

A TREATISE OF THE TRUE MILLENNIUM SHEWING

That it is not a Reign of Persons raised from the Dead,[1] but of the Church flourishing gloriously for a thousand Years after the Conversion of the Jews, and the flowing in of all Nations to them thus converted to the Christian Faith....[2]

... I proceed now to show, in what things I agree with the assertors of that doctrine, and how far I find myself constrained, by the force of truth, to differ from them.

I. I believe, then, that, after the fall of Antichrist, there shall be such a glorious state of the church, by the conversion of the Jews to the Christian faith, as shall be to it life from the dead; that it shall then flourish in peace and plenty, in righteousness and holiness, and in a pious offspring; that then shall begin a glorious and undisturbed reign of Christ over both Jew and Gentile, to continue a thousand years during the time of Satan's bonding....[3]

1. I agree with the patrons of the Millennium in this, that I believe Satan hath not yet been bound a thousand years, nor will he be so bound till the time of the calling of the Jews, and the time of St. John's Millennium.

(continued on page 95)

<u>**4**</u> Instead of Jesus himself, the church, consisting largely of converted Jews, would reign.

<u>**5**</u> The rebuilding of the temple in the millennial Jerusalem becomes a critical factor in nineteenth-century developments in eschatology and still informs popular visions of the end times today.

<u>**6**</u> Whitby affirms the classic Christian doctrine that the church replaced Judaism in God's plan for the world. According to this teaching, Jewish religious and cultic practices became obsolete with the (first) coming of Christ; instead, Christ, "the Lamb, shall be their temple." This contrasts sharply with later dispensational developments in eschatological teaching.

<u>**7**</u> This recalls some of the ancient beliefs of the millennium as a time of lavish payback for the trials and sufferings of the persecuted and martyred saints.

2. I agree with them in this, that the true Millennium will not begin till the fall of Antichrist; nor will the Jews be converted till that time, the idolatry of the Roman church being one great obstacle of their conversion.

3. I agree both with the modern and the ancient millenaries, that then shall be great peace and plenty, and great measures of knowledge and of righteousness in the whole church of God.

I therefore only differ from the ancient millenaries in three things:

1. In denying Christ's personal reign upon earth during this thousand years....**4**

2. Though I dare not absolutely deny ... that the city of Jerusalem shall be then rebuilt, and the converted Jews shall return to it, ... yet do I confidently deny ... that the temple of Jerusalem shall be then built again:**5** for this is contrary not only to the plain declaration of St. John, who saith, I saw no temple in this new Jerusalem (Rev. xxi. 22), whence I infer, there is to be no temple in any part of it; but to the whole design of the epistle to the Hebrews, which is to shew the dissolution of the temple-service, for the weakness and unprofitableness of it; that the Jewish tabernacle was only a fixture of the true and the more perfect tabernacle which the Lord pitched, and not man; the Jewish sanctuary only a worldly sanctuary, a pattern and a fixture of the heavenly one into which Christ our High Priest is entered**6** (Heb. viii. 2. ix. 2, 11, 23, 24). Now, such a temple, such a sanctuary, and such service, cannot be suitable to the most glorious and splendid times of the Christian church; and therefore the apostle saith, The Lord God omnipotent, and the Lamb, shall be their temple.

3. I differ both from the ancient and modern millenaries, as far as they assert that this shall be a reign of such Christians as have suffered under the Heathen persecutors,**7** or by the rage of Antichrist; making it only a reign of the converted Jews, and of the Gentiles then flowing in to them, and uniting into one church with them. This I believe to be indeed the truth of this mistaken doctrine.

◆ During the eighteenth century, Whitby's eschatology proved to be quite popular, and several noteworthy commentaries on Revelation advanced the same view. One of the most brilliant American philosophers and theologians of all times, Jonathan Edwards (1703–58), best known to students of American literature as the author of the sermon "Sinners in the Hands of an Angry God," also adopted postmillennialism.

For three decades he kept a journal on the book of Revelation in which he analyzed its contents, took notes from commentators, and recorded the signs of the times that he believed were leading to the millennium. He also set forth his millennial ideas in books and sermons. These materials, which grew out of the revivals of the Great Awakening of the 1740s, revealed a postmillennial vision for the landscape of the New World.

8 Catholicism and Islam, respectively. During the millennial period, Edwards argued, heresy, infidelity, and superstition would be eliminated; Islam destroyed; the Jews converted; and the heathen of Africa, America, and India won to Christ.

9 In his writings, Edwards stated that the church would achieve a golden age on earth through the process of preaching the gospel in the power of the Holy Spirit. The destruction of the Antichrist, whom he identified with the pope, would usher in this period.

10 That is, the pope. Despite postmillennialism's broadened and somewhat more optimistic vision, it retained premillennialism's profound acrimony toward Catholicism.

Jonathan Edwards

from A History of the Work of Redemption

The two great works of the devil which he in this space of time wrought against the kingdom of Christ, are his creating his Antichristian and Mahometan kingdoms,[8] which have been, and still are, two kingdoms of great extent and strength, both together swallowing up the ancient Roman Empire; the kingdom of Antichrist swallowing up the Western empire, and Satan's Mahometan kingdom the Eastern empire. As the scriptures in the book of Revelation represent it, it is in the destruction of these that the glorious victory of Christ, at the introduction of the glorious times of the church, will mainly consist.[9] And here let us briefly observe how Satan erects and maintains these two great kingdoms of his in opposition to the kingdom of Christ.

With respect to the kingdom of Antichrist. This seems to be the masterpiece of all the contrivances of the devil against the kingdom of Christ, and is evidently so spoken of in scripture, and therefore Antichrist is the man of sin, or that man of sin (2 Thes. 2:3).[10] He is so called emphatically, as though he were so eminently. So he is called Antichrist, which signifies the opponent or adversary of Christ. Not that he is the only opponent of Christ; there were many others besides him. The Apostle John observes, that in his days there were many Antichrists. But yet this is called the Antichrist, as though there were none but he, because he was so eminently, and above all others. So this contrivance of the devil, is called the mystery of iniquity (2 Thes. 2:7). And we find no enemy of Christ one half so much spoken of in the prophecies of Revelation as this; and the destruction of no enemy is spoken of as so glorious and happy for the church. The craft and subtlety of the devil, above all appears in this work of his; as might be shown, were it not that it would consume too much time.

(continued on page 99)

11 It was papal oppression that had forced people into superstition and ignorance and had taken the Bible out of the hands of laypeople. Fortunately, the Protestant Reformation had resulted in the reestablishment of sound doctrine, the propagation of the gospel to the heathen, and the revival of learning.

12 Edwards calculated from Revelation 16:1 that the papacy would continue in power for 1,260 years and then expire either in 1866 or 2016, depending on which date one selected as the point at which the institution came into existence. At that time, a great outpouring of the Holy Spirit would destroy the Antichrist. A revival resulting from the preaching of the gospel would overthrow Satan's visible kingdom, the apostate church, and a great age of human happiness would follow. He saw himself as living in momentous times, as the Great Awakening was taking place around him. He argued that the scriptural prophecies of the "latter-day outpouring of the Spirit" applied to America.

13 The holiness and commitment to Christ of this age would be accompanied by a vast increase in knowledge and learning. International peace and understanding would prevail, and along with it would come the greatest prosperity the world had ever known. It would also be a time when Christianity and the church would be the most respected institutions in society.

At the close of the millennial age, much of the world would fall away from Christ and his church. Gog and Magog would be able to recruit vast numbers for their armies because people had abused the prosperity of the era to serve lust and corruption. But then Christ would come, crush the rebellion, and carry out the last judgment. The church would be caught up in the clouds to meet its Lord in the air, the world would be set on fire, and it would become a great furnace in which the enemies of Christ would be tormented forever.

Edwards's emphasis on evangelism and the importance of a biblically educated laity found an acute significance in the nineteenth century. To these postmillennialists, the rapid spread of evangelism across the globe was not just a sure sign of Christ's coming kingdom, it was also a tool to be used to help usher in the millennium.

This is a contrivance of the devil to turn the ministry of the Christian church into a ministry of the devil, and to turn these angels of the churches into fallen angels, and so into devils. And in the tyranny, and superstition, and idolatry, and persecution, which he set up, he contrives to make an image of ancient Paganism, and more than to restore what was lost in the empire by the overthrow of Paganism in the time of Constantine....

During this time, also superstition and ignorance more and more prevailed. The holy scriptures by degrees were taken out of the hands of the laity, the better to promote the unscriptural and wicked designs of the Pope and the clergy; and instead of promoting knowledge among the people, they industriously promoted ignorance.[11] It was a received maxim among them, that ignorance is the mother of devotion: and so great was the darkness of those times, that learning was almost extinct in the world. The very priests themselves, most of them, were barbarously ignorant as to any commendable learning, or any other knowledge, than their hellish craft in oppressing and tyrannizing over the souls of the people. The superstition and wickedness of the church of Rome, kept growing worse and worse till the very time of the Reformation; and the whole Christian world were led away into this great deception....

... The visible kingdom of Satan shall be overthrown, and the kingdom of Christ set up on the ruins of it, everywhere throughout the whole habitable globe.[12] Now shall the promise made to Abraham be fulfilled, That "in him and in his seed all the families of the earth shall be blessed;" and Christ now shall become the desire of all nations, agreeable to Haggai 2:7. Now the kingdom of Christ shall in the most strict and literal sense be extended to all nations, and the whole earth. There are many passages of Scripture that can be understood in no other sense. What can be more universal than that in Is. 11:9: "For the earth shall be full of the knowledge of the Lord, as the waters cover the sea."[13]

◆ Despite the popularity of postmillennial teaching in the eighteenth and nineteenth centuries, the number of premillennialists increased markedly as the French Revolution fostered a renewed interest in prophecy and speculation about the end of the world. This was particularly so because Roman Catholic power in France had been destroyed. During the revolution, church properties were seized, including the papal territory at Avignon, many priests were sent to the guillotine, a "religion of reason" was founded, and the pope was exiled from Rome. Because they believed the millennium would not come until the papacy had been destroyed, many Bible scholars concluded that the end of the age was near. They believed they were witnessing the "deadly wound" inflicted on the papacy as foretold in Revelation 13, and their calculations of biblical numbers seemed to point to their age as the decisive period for the establishment of the millennium.

Great Britain was the center of the new prophetic movement. Believers were not only convinced that Christ would return to set up the millennium, they were also concerned about the conversion of the Jews and their return to the Holy land, a significant development that continues to inform Christian Zionist perspectives in the twenty-first century.

In the Untied States, postmillennialism remained strong during the nineteenth century, where it was often associated with patriotism. A conservative version posited that God's power over his enemies will become more fully manifest as the time of Christ's return draws near, and their teaching became a motivating force in the great foreign missionary outreach. But a liberal postmillennialism was also gaining ground as the new century approached. The primary source of this optimistic approach was not the scriptures but the merging of the eighteenth-century view of human goodness with the nineteenth-century myth of progress.

1 Despite the popularity of the postmillennial view, premillennialism continued and was brought to greater prominence through the work of John Nelson Darby (1800–1882). Darby's insistence that these teachings are not some "strange speculation" is an example of the populist approach to the topic emphasized by preachers and teachers of this time.

7 □ Nineteenth-century Dispensationalism

John N. Darby

from *Lectures on the Second Coming*

LECTURE I.
(I THESSALONIANS I.)

And now our hearts should understand ... that the coming of Christ is not some strange speculation, or the advanced idea of a few,[1] but was set before the church as elementary and foundation truth, and formed a part of all their habits and feelings, and mingled itself with every thought. It was and is the keystone of all that keeps up the heart in this solitary place, (looking at it as journeying through the wilderness,) and with a heart full of love for God, and the desire to see Christ, we can appreciate the apostle's prayer for us: "The Lord direct your hearts into the love of God, and into the patient waiting for Christ." We have not long to wait, and it is worth being patient for.

... He comes to receive them to Himself, that where He is there they may be also, to change their vile bodies and fashion them like His glorious body. For the saints the resurrection is a resurrection of life, not of judgment. It is a raising in glory, or changing into it by the Lord's power, those that are already quickened and justified....

(continued on page 103)

2   The fundamental concern is the status of the individual before God, not, as in past eras, one's church or denominational affiliation. In fact, the true church of Christ was in no way the same as the official church establishment, or the "professing church," as dispensationalists liked to label it. The true church was that body of believers, the "invisible church," who found Christ personally through faith, and they alone would pass through the final judgment and enter into eternal life.

3   Darby leverages this doctrine not just as a source of comfort for believers but also as an explicit tool for evangelism.

4   The teaching that Jerusalem—in a newly restored state of Israel—will be the center of activity in the end times becomes increasingly important in premillennialist thinking in the nineteenth century and beyond.

... The moment I get hold of the truth that the coming is, for believers,[2] to receive them to Himself, the moment I see that His coming the second time is to bring in the glory, to change us into His own likeness and to have us with Him, it affects everything, instead of being an unimportant thing. I believe death is the most blessed thing that can happen to a man; but is not the thing I am looking for. I am looking to see Him. He might come tomorrow, or tonight, or now. If He did, don't you think it would spoil all your plans? Suppose you thought He might come, would it not make a difference in your thoughts? You know it would.[3]

LECTURE IV.
(ROMANS XI.)

Of the two great subjects besides our individual salvation, of which the Scriptures treat, as already stated, namely, the church, and the government of the world, the latter leads us at once to the Jews as its centre, as the church is of the heavenly glory under Christ; under whom, as their Head, all things in heaven and earth are to be gathered together in one. That government will extend over the whole earth, but the royal nation and seat and centre of government will be the Jewish people. To Jerusalem, as the centre alike of worship and government, all nations will flow....[4]

(continued on page 105)

5   That is, the Jewish people.

6   Darby objects to the long-held doctrine that Christianity wholly supplanted Judaism in God's plan for the world. Instead, Darby recognizes the Jewish people as both the historical Israel and the object of the Hebrew Bible prophecies concerning the restoration of the Davidic kingdom in the end times. Both Jews and Christians still have a role to play.

Darby's immense contribution to the study of eschatology was both this new *specific* interpretation of the second coming and an entirely new *method* of interpreting the Bible that allowed it. Developed in the 1830s, this new method was taught by a group Darby led, the Plymouth Brethren. Called "dispensationalists," they taught that God's plan unfolded throughout the ages in distinct phases, or dispensations, each uniquely marked by the manner in which God related to humanity at that time. The Bible was to be taken literally with the understanding that what might have been true in one dispensation may not be equally as true in another—some of God's earlier promises may appear to be suspended during a different dispensation—but that in the end, all of God's promises would be fulfilled. Likewise, prophecies given in one dispensation may have their final fulfillment in a later dispensation, possibly in a manner that even the original prophet may not have comprehended. This interpretative strategy simultaneously allowed for the primacy of Christianity, affirmed the continued importance of Judaism in God's plan, and helped harmonize the various, and sometimes perplexing, apocalyptic texts found throughout the Bible.

The dispensational perspective fell on fertile ground among evangelicals in nineteenth-century America. Darby's books on eschatological themes became quite popular in the English-speaking world, and his influence reverberated through the leading prophecy teachers of the time and continue to resonate today.

The difficulty we have to meet in men's minds on this point is this: that that people[5] having been set aside for their sins—first of idolatry, secondly, the rejection of the Lord Jesus—and the church and kingdom of heaven having been established, it is supposed they will not be restored, but merge in the profession of Christianity.[6] But this sets aside alike the prophecies of the Old and the declarations of the New Testament....

In the 25th verse, he adds, "For I would not, brethren, that ye should be ignorant of this mystery ... that blindness in part is happened to Israel, until the fullness of the Gentiles be come in. And so all Israel shall be saved, as it is written, There shall come out of Zion the Deliverer, and shall turn away ungodliness from Jacob." They are partially set aside till the church be called, and then a Deliverer, Christ, shall, after all the church is brought in, come out of Zion, and turn away their ungodliness. This is not by the gospel as now preached, for he adds, "As touching the gospel, they are enemies for your sakes," the Gentiles being thus let in: "but as touching the election, they are beloved for the fathers' sakes. For the gifts and calling of God are without repentance."

Here we have God's way towards them clearly set forth. Partial blindness for a time, during which the church, the fullness of the Gentiles, is called: when that is closed, their Deliverer comes out of Zion. Our gospel is not the means, they are as a nation enemies as respects that: but they have not ceased to be beloved for the fathers' sakes. That is a matter of God's election, and as to His gifts and dealings He does not change His mind.

◆ Dispensationalists were avid supporters of Zionism, but most were satisfied to be mere observers of the movement. They seldom became politically involved in promoting its goals. There was an early exception to this rule, however, in the person of William E. Blackstone (1841–1935). A lifelong Methodist, he did not attend college or receive any formal ministerial training, but he was a polished author with a thorough knowledge of the scriptures, and during the 1870s he moved in a social circle that included several prominent dispensationalists, among them D. L. Moody, and he lectured widely on Christ's imminent return. In 1891, Blackstone single-handedly drew up a petition to President Benjamin Harrison that urged him to gain international consent for the granting of Palestine as a haven for persecuted Russian Jews.

7 The Jews were central to Blackstone's thought. The Jewish tradition— their beliefs, laws, and rituals—had merely kept them waiting for the Messiah and the reestablishment of their national home in Palestine. They would fulfill the role God had intended for human history. Nevertheless, Blackstone believed strongly that Jews could only find salvation in Christ. He taught that the Jews in Palestine would accept Jesus during the great tribulation, whereas all deviant Christians and non-Protestant groups would surely be consigned to eternal damnation.

Blackstone also viewed reformed and liberal or assimilated Jews quite negatively. He maintained that they had turned their back on their role in the divine plan for the end times. Because most of them did not favor the Zionist program, he assumed they would not participate in the national restoration, and because they were resistant to evangelical missionary efforts, they would surely perish.

William E. Blackstone

The Blackstone Memorial, 1891:

PRESENTED TO THE PRESIDENT OF THE UNITED STATES IN
FAVOR OF THE RESTORATION OF PALESTINE TO THE JEWS.

What shall be done for the Russian Jews? It is both unwise and useless to
undertake to dictate to Russia concerning her internal affairs. The Jews
have lived as foreigners in her dominions for centuries and she fully
believes that they are a burden upon her resources and prejudicial to the
welfare of her peasant population, and will not allow them to remain.
She is determined that they must go. Hence, like the Sephardim of
Spain, these Ashkenazim must emigrate. But where shall 2,000,000 of
such poor people go? Europe is crowded and has not room for more
peasant population. Shall they come to America? This will be a
tremendous expense, and require years.

Why not give Palestine back to them again?[7] According to God's
distribution of nations it is their home, an inalienable possession from
which they were expelled by force. Under their cultivation it was a
remarkably fruitful land sustaining millions of Israelites who industrially
tilled its hillsides and valleys. They were agriculturists and producers as
well as a nation of great commercial importance—the center of
civilization and religion.

Why shall not the powers which under the treaty of Berlin, in
1878, gave Bulgaria to the Bulgarians and Servia to the Servians now
give Palestine back to the Jews? These provinces, as well as Roumainia,
Montenegro and Greece, were wrested from the Turks and given to
their natural owners. Does not Palestine as rightfully belong to the Jews?
It is said that rains are increasing and there are evidences that the land
is recovering its ancient fertility. If they could have autonomy in
government the Jews of the world would rally to transport and establish
their suffering brethren in their time-honored habitation. For over
seventeen centuries they have patiently waited for such an opportunity.

(continued on page 109)

8 Blackstone believed the United States had a special role to play in carrying out the divine plan for humanity. America was the modern-day Cyrus who would assist in the Jewish restoration to the Promised Land, and it would be judged according to how it carried out this divine assignment. He secured signatures from 414 noted Americans, including political officials, clergymen, journalists, and big businessmen, but the federal government did nothing about it.

◆ Blackstone is significant because he was the earliest dispensationalist who sought to influence the American government to support Zionism—a tradition that has continued to the present among dispensational supporters of Israel. However, his primary motivation was not the physical and national survival of the Jews but rather the establishment of the Jewish state, which was needed to prepare the way for the coming of the Messiah, Jesus Christ, and the millennial kingdom.

They have not become agriculturists elsewhere because they believed they were mere sojourners in the various nations, and were yet to return to Palestine and till their own land. Whatever vested rights by possession may have accrued to Turkey can be easily compensated, possibly by the Jews assuming an equitable portion of the national debt.

We believe this is an appropriate time for all nations and especially the Christian nations of Europe to show kindness to Israel. A million exiles, by their terrible suffering, are piteously appealing to our sympathy, justice, and humanity. Let us now restore to them the land of which they were so cruelly despoiled by our Roman ancestors.

To this end we respectfully petition His Excellency Benjamin Harrison, President of the United States,[8] and the Honorable James G. Blaine, Secretary of State, to use their good offices and influence with the Governments of their Imperial Majesties—

Alexander III, Czar of Russia;

Victoria, Queen of Great Britain and Empress of India;

William II, Emperor of Germany;

Francis Joseph, Emperor of Austria-Hungary;

Abdul Hamid II, Sultan of Turkey;

His Royal Majesty, Humbert, King of Italy;

Her Royal Majesty Marie Christiana, Queen Regent of Spain;

And the Government of the Republic of France and with the Governments of Belgium, Holland, Denmark, Sweden, Portugal, Roumania, Servia, Bulgaria and Greece. To secure the holding at any early date, of an international conference to consider the condition of the Israelites and their claims to Palestine as their ancient home, and to promote, in all other just and proper ways, the alleviation of their suffering condition.

[Followed by approximately 400 additional signatures.]

9 Blackstone was also fascinated with current events and their potential to be signs of the fast-approaching end. He quoted from a range of prophetic biblical texts and saw their fulfillment in the marvels of modern life. Hence, Blackstone believed, Christ's return was surely imminent.

10 Impressive numbers for Blackstone's time.

from *Jesus Is Coming*

CHAPTER XXII
SIGNS OF CHRIST'S SPEEDY COMING.

We believe that the coming of our Lord is to be personal and premillennial, also, that it is imminent. Let us remember the admonition that we must distinguish between the rapture—His coming into the air to receive His saints (1 Thes. 4), which may occur at any moment—and the Revelation—His coming down to the earth with His saints—which latter will not occur until after the preaching of the gospel as a witness (Matt. 24:14), the gathering of Israel, in unbelief, the manifestation of Antichrist, and other prophesied events. Now we are to consider, what are the evidences for also believing that His coming, the Rapture, is near? Out of many reasons we will give [several], as follows:[9]

I. The Prevalence of Travel and Knowledge.
"Shut up the words and seal the book even to the time of the end: many shall run to and fro and knowledge shall be increased" (Dan. 12:4).

A comparison of recent years with the present shows a most marvelous increase in both travel and knowledge....

Now, invention has chained the mighty forces of steam and electricity to palatial carriages by land and sea, so that one can go around the world, with comfort and ease, in sixty days.

Railways cover the earth and steamers track the sea like a mighty spider's web.

Our text says, Many shall run to and fro. In the year 1896 the number of passengers carried on the railroads in the United States was 525,120,756 and the mileage was 13,054,840,243, and in the whole world the railroad passengers were 2,384,000,000 and the mileage 28,677,000,000. Add to this the travel by steamers and private conveyance, the explorations into every conceivable corner of the earth, from the equator to the poles, and the enormous aggregate is surely a literal fulfillment of this sign of the end....[10]

(continued on page 113)

[11] Recent natural disasters are often seen as a certain sign of the end.

[12] Written prior to World War I, this observation proved to be all too prophetic.

II. Perilous Times.

"This know also that in the last days perilous times shall come" (2 Tim. 3:1).

   a. Physically: Pestilence, famine, earthquake, cyclones, etc.

Possibly the recently vented oil and gases of the earth are a preparation for some mighty conflagration to be aided by newly manifested heat and electrical forces from the sun (2 Thes. 2:8).[11]

   b. Politically and Socially.

Under this head we need only refer to the progress of Nihilism, Socialism, Communism and Anarchy. Could there be anything worse than the creed of the latter, viz.: The first lie is God and the second is Law. They openly avow that their mission is to destroy the present social structure, and they prophesy (perhaps with the accuracy of Caiaphas), that something better will come.

   c. Distress of Nations.

National jealousies have caused offensive and defensive preparations on a scale of such magnitude as to literally grind out the life of the people with oppressive taxation.

All Europe is practically a soldiers' camp, with 23,000,000 drilled men ready to fly at each other in a universal war, with weapons so ingenious and deadly as to put all the past record beneath the shadow of comparison....

It is appalling to contemplate the woe and carnage that would follow in the wake of these forces, if once let loose....[12]

(continued on page 115)

13 He also identifies the growth in America of other sects and religions, such as Theosophy, Christian Science, and Buddhism, as "delusions" and "sign[s] that the end is near."

14 This apostasy also included emerging modern methods of scriptural interpretation, including higher criticism, which challenged fundamental premillennialist and dispensationalist assumptions about the Bible and its meaning.

15 Blackstone's age was one of unprecedented global missionary energy and activity.

III. Spiritualism.

"Now the Spirit speaketh expressly that in the latter times some shall depart from the faith, giving heed to seducing spirits and doctrines of devils" (1 Tim. 4:1).

Modern Spiritualism is by no means mere trickery. There is plenty of fraud and deception that requires darkened rooms and suspicious cabinets, but there are also unquestionable mysteries and spirit manifestations, demons that long to possess the bodies of men, wicked spirits which love darkness rather than light.

It is a definite sign of the times....[13]

IV. Apostacy.

The day of the Lord (the revelation), shall not come, "except there come a falling away first" (2 Thes. 2:3)....

Post-Millennialists say very little about the coming of the Lord. An elderly Methodist clergyman in Florida said that he had heard only five sermons on the Lord's coming, and he preached them all himself. In many large audiences where an expression has been taken it is surprising to see what a great majority have never heard a single sermon on this Blessed Hope, which finds so large a place in the Holy Scriptures.

There is a notable dearth of power in the preaching of the Word today! Men descant on how to reach the masses but the masses go on unreached.[14]

V. World-wide Evangelism.

"This gospel of the kingdom shall be preached in all the world for a witness to all nations, then shall the end come" (Matt. 24:14)....

Every nation in the world today has a testimony ... with the exception of Tibet, Nepaul and Bhotan and the Mohammedan countries of Afghanistan and the Soudan, and into the former the Bible has already gone in great numbers, and missionaries stand at the doors waiting the privilege of entering in....[15]

(continued on page 117)

16 Above all, Blackstone emphasized the restoration of the Jews to the Holy Land, which he called "God's sun-dial."

◆ The image of the "sun-dial" is one of steady progession, but Blackstone believed that history was divided into distinct phases. "The end of this dispensation" was not to be accomplished gradually, but rather triggered, followed by the rapid ushering in of the next phase of existence on the earth, in which God would deal with humanity in a new way.

VII. Israel.

God's sun-dial.[16]

If we want to know our place in chronology, our position in the march of events, look at Israel....

Israel shall be restored to Palestine and no more be pulled up out of their land (Amos 9:15)....

Jerusalem was to be trodden down until the times of the Gentiles be fulfilled.

But note carefully that a little later Jesus said, "Now learn a parable of the fig tree (and all the trees): when her branch is yet tender, and putteth forth leaves, ye know that summer is near. So likewise, ye, in like manner, when ye shall see these things come to pass, know that it is nigh, even at the doors" (Mark 13:28; Luke 21:29)....

Now if Israel is beginning to show signs of national life and is actually returning to Palestine, then surely the end of this dispensation "is nigh, even at the doors."

◆ Many of the leading evangelists of the nineteenth and twentieth centuries were dispensationalists, the most prominent being Dwight L. Moody and Billy Graham. Moody (1837–99) was born in Northfield, Massachusetts, and had little formal education.

Though he was only a layman with no theological training, his reputation as a preacher grew rapidly, and before long he was in demand all over America. He remains one of the most renowned and influential preachers America has ever produced.

Critical to Moody's success was organization. He refused to come to a city until all the ministers in the evangelical churches invited him. A local committee was set up to care for all the arrangements, such as securing a hall, advertising, and fund-raising. A volunteer choir was assembled and drilled in rehearsal. Ushers were chosen and trained along with "inquiry room workers," ministers and laymen who counseled those who came forward to receive Christ. During the campaign, Moody also held workshops for Christian workers who would play an important role in the "follow-up" of the converts.

His manner as a preacher was a model of decorum. He dressed like an ordinary businessman, the meetings were carefully planned and run according to a schedule, and he spoke calmly and plainly. His messages were simple and to the point, and he focused on God, sin, and one's need for a Savior. Moody did not dwell on theology, but he was the first major American revivalist to adopt premillennialism. He viewed himself as first and foremost a winner of souls, and his emotionally powerful sermons were designed to achieve this objective. As for the converts, his advice to them was to join a local church right away and get to work for God.

17 Moody recognized the danger of speculation and took a more modest approach than many of his fellow dispensationalists: though we cannot specify the date, Jesus will certainly return soon.

18 The point is not to hypothesize about the exact date, but rather to let Christ's imminent return goad the believer into an urgent awareness. This diligence is a requisite for the Christian life, according to Moody.

Dwight L. Moody

from *The Second Coming of Christ*

I do not know why people should not like to study the Bible, and find out all about this precious doctrine of our Lord's return. Some have gone beyond prophecy, and tried to tell the very day He would come. Perhaps that is one reason why people don't believe this doctrine. He is coming—we know that; but just when He is coming we don't know.[17] Matthew settles that: "But of that day and hour knoweth no man, no, not the angels of heaven, but my Father only." The angels don't know. It is something the Father keeps to Himself....

If Christ had said, "I will not come back for 2,000 years," none of His disciples would have begun to watch for Him until the time was near, but it is

THE PROPER ATTITUDE OF A CHRISTIAN

to be always looking for his Lord's return. So God does not tell us when Christ is to come, but He tells us to watch. Just as Simeon and Anna watched and waited for His first coming, so should true believers watch and wait for His return. It is not enough to say you are a Christian, and that you are all right. You are not all right unless you obey the command to watch.[18]

We find also that He is to come unexpectedly and suddenly. "For as the lightning cometh out of the east and shineth unto the west, even so shall also the coming of the Son of man be." And again, "Therefore be ye also ready, for in such an hour as ye think not the Son of man cometh."...

THE FIRST THING HE IS TO DO

is to take His Church out of the world. He calls the Church His bride, and He says He is going to prepare a place for her. We may judge, says one, what a glorious place it will be from the length of time He is in preparing it, and when the place is ready He will come and take the Church to Himself....

(continued on page 121)

19 The postmillennialist position.

20 Moody refers to the parable found in Matthew 25:1–13 where Jesus likens the time of his return to ten virgins, each with a small oil lamp, waiting for the bridegroom. Not knowing when the bridegroom would arrive, the five wise virgins prepared themselves by obtaining a supply of oil for their lamps, but the five foolish virgins did not. At midnight when the bridegroom arrived, the five wise virgins lit their lamps and were welcomed into the wedding banquet; the five foolish virgins were found unprepared and the bridegroom turned them away, saying, "Verily I say unto you, I know you not."

21 Likewise, the postmillennialist position.

22 That is, *only* a spiritual reign. Moody is contrasting the postmillennial spiritualized understanding with his own belief that Christ's thousand-year reign will be an *actual* kingdom.

... He has prepared a mansion for His bride, the Church, and He promises for our joy and comfort that

HE WILL COME HIMSELF

and bring us to the place He has been all this while preparing.

There was a time when I used to mourn that I should not be alive in the millennium; but now

I EXPECT TO BE IN THE MILLENNIUM....

Some people say, "I believe Christ will come on the other side of the millennium."[19]

Where do they get it? I can't find it. The Word of God nowhere tells me to watch and wait for signs of the coming of the millennium, (such as the return of the Jews), but for the coming of the Lord; to be ready at midnight to meet Him, like those five wise virgins.[20]

At one time I thought the world would grow better and better until Christ could stay away no longer;[21] but in studying the Bible I don't find anyplace where God says so, or that Christ is to have a spiritual reign on earth of a thousand years.[22] I find that

THE WORLD IS TO GROW WORSE AND WORSE,

and that at length there is going to be a separation: "Two women grinding at a mill; one taken and the other left. Two men in one bed; one taken and the other left." The Church is to be translated out of the world....

(continued on page 123)

23 One of Moody's primary uses of this doctrine was to stir souls to salvation. The evangelistic technique of pointing out the dire suffering in store for those not rescued by Christ before the tribulation is familiar to those who have seen the well-known 1972 film *A Thief in the Night* or its sequels.

24 Moody closed his meetings with an altar call, a challenge and an invitation to receive Christ and become a Christian. This practice has been followed by countless preachers and revivalists, including, perhaps most famously, Billy Graham.

Now, some think this is a new and strange doctrine, and that they who preach it are speckled birds. But let me say that many spiritual men in the pulpits of Great Britain, as well as in this country are firm in this faith. Spurgeon preached it. I have heard Newman Hall say that he knew no reason why Christ might not come before he got through with his sermon. But in certain churches, where they have the form of godliness, but deny the power thereof—just the state of things which Paul declares shall be in the last days—this doctrine is not preached or believed. They do not want sinners to cry out in their meetings, "What must I do to be saved?"[23] They want intellectual preachers who will cultivate their taste, brilliant preachers who will rouse their imagination, but they don't want the preaching that has in it the power of the Holy Ghost. We live in the day of

SHAMS IN RELIGION.

The Church is cold and formal; may God wake us up! And I know of no better way to do it than to get the Church to look for the return of our Lord....

"Behold, I come quickly," said Christ to John. Three times it is repeated in the last chapter of the Bible. And almost the closing words of the Bible are the prayer: "Even so, come, Lord Jesus." Were the early Christians disappointed, then? No; no man is disappointed who obeys the voice of God. The world waited for the first coming of the Lord, waited for 4,000 years, and then He came. He was here only thirty-three years, and then He went away. But he left us a promise that He would come again; and, as the world watched and waited for His first coming and did not watch in vain, so now to them who wait for His appearing, shall He appear a second time unto salvation.

Now, let the question go around, "Am I ready to meet the Lord if He comes tonight?"[24]

◆ A contemporary of William E. Blackstone, Cyrus Ingerson Scofield (1843–1921) was the other great popularizer of dispensational premillennialism. Born in Michigan, he moved with his family to Lebanon, Tennessee, where he was raised an Episcopalian. After Civil War service in the Confederate army, he went to Kansas, where he became a lawyer and an elected official. He fell victim to alcohol, which wrecked his marriage, but sometime around 1880 while in prison he was converted and became a Congregationalist minister. Although he had no theological training, he took over a Congregational mission church in Dallas, Texas, and was ordained in 1882. He taught himself dispensationalism, began a correspondence Bible study course, and in 1885 published *Rightly Dividing the Word of Truth*, a book that established his credentials as an advocate of premillennialism.

After building the Dallas congregation into a prospering church, in 1895 he went to Northfield, Massachusetts, to pastor the local Congregational church, work with Dwight L. Moody, and engage in Bible conference ministry. In 1902 he returned to the Dallas church and labored on a reference Bible project that became his legacy, a work of monumental influence on eschatological understanding from the time of its publication through today. His study Bible is still in print.

1 The following detailed exposition of the seven-year tribulation period is representative of the elaborate schemas Scofield's studies yielded.

2 Scofield rejects the more optimistic postmillennial view in no uncertain terms. History is not evolving upward, but is leading inexorably downward toward a cycle of cataclysmic events as foretold by the prophets.

8 □ Twentieth-century Developments

Cyrus I. Scofield

from *Addresses on Prophecy*

THE GREAT TRIBULATION

The next prophetic period we are to consider is the "great tribulation."...[1]

I invite your attention first of all to the following words of our Lord which form part of that discourse called, from the place where it was spoken, "The Olivet Discourse":

"For then shall be great tribulation, such as was not since the beginning of the world to this time, no, nor ever shall be. And except those days should be shortened, there should no flesh be saved: but for the elect's sake those days shall be shortened" (Matt. 24:21, 22).

Many other references to this period of unexampled woe are found in the prophecies.

Now, before I enter upon this special subject, permit me, first of all, to recall to those of you who have been following this series of addresses on prophetical truth the two or three things which have been established....

The first proposition was that this age ends in catastrophe; this age ends in judgment; this age ends in woe; not, as some would have us believe, by the gradual process of evolution, lifting the race higher and higher until it passes by insensible gradations, into a state of blessedness and peace, but in sudden and awful ruin, making necessary a complete reconstruction of human government, and of the whole social economy of the earth.[2]

3 Scofield's influence on the fundamentalist movement in the twentieth century was enormous. His writings made dispensationalism a dogmatic standard in the Bible institute movement in North America, which established institutions that provided practical training for laypeople who wished to become "full-time Christian workers." By 1945, more than one hundred Bible institutes had been founded, although some were rather ephemeral. They also served the interdenominational fundamentalist movement like the headquarters of a denomination, and by the mid-twentieth century they were the prime source of evangelical Protestant missionary recruits. The heart of the instructional program was the Bible taught in English translation (not in the original Hebrew and Greek), and it was almost invariably taught from a dispensationalist perspective.

As to the events in which this present dispensation ends,[3] you will remember that we saw from the First Epistle to the Thessalonians, chapter 4:16–18, that the first in the succession of these events is the taking away from the earth of all who are Christ's, that is to say, of the real church composed of true believers since the crucifixion.

"The Lord himself," says Paul, "shall descend from Heaven with a shout, with the voice of the archangel, and with the trump of God: and the dead in Christ shall rise first."...

The second point which I trust has been established by that which has gone before, and of which I will remind you so that we may have the ground clear, is that the end of this age is not the end of the world....

The world, then, does not end for more than 1000 years after this age ends. The tribulation and the millennium must run their course first....

We come now to our Lord's prediction of a time of unexampled tribulation....

(*continued on page 129*)

4 Scofield's most important achievement was *The Scofield Reference Bible*, which expounded the dispensationalist distinctives he had been preaching on the Bible conference circuit. It was published in 1909 by Oxford University Press and became the most widely used work that propagated dispensationalism. It was revised and expanded in 1917 and updated in 1967, and over the years more than ten million copies have been sold. Using the King James Version, Scofield embellished it with an extensive system of chain references and footnotes that largely followed the eschatological teaching of John Nelson Darby. Had Scofield presented his explanatory notes in a separate commentary, they would have probably gone unnoticed. As it was, however, the notes were printed in a manner that a person would read them as he or she studied the Bible, allowing them to "fill in the details from portions of scripture elsewhere."

Decades before the current fascination with specialty or niche study Bibles, Scofield's influential work gave millions of readers a sense of authority as they learned to view the scriptures through the dispensational system. Simply put, *The Scofield Reference Bible* did more than any other printed work to anchor dispensational premillennialism in American fundamentalism. The Scofield notes became so dominant within evangelical circles that many adherents considered the commentary the true interpretation of the Bible, thus implicitly granting it the status of equal authority with the biblical text itself. In fact, for many evangelicals, the Scofield notes possessed what amounted to de facto canonicity. Critics never tire of pointing out that the very people who say they can read the Bible for themselves all too often end up poring over Scofield's notes to discover what the text "really" means.

5 Although the earth is on the cusp of entering these final days, some godly entity is temporarily preventing it. When that restraint is removed, the church will be removed from the earth, and all hell will break loose.

... He declares that the time of trouble of which He speaks shall be a time of greater trouble than anything which the earth will see until it comes to pass. We have, then, in our Lord's prediction alone a fearful prophecy even if we were unable to fill in the details from portions of scripture elsewhere.[4]

But our Lord's prediction does not stand alone. Not to speak of the abundant testimony of the Old Testament prophets, out of which I have already given citations, we have in the New Testament considerably more than half of the last of its books devoted to the details of this period....

The entire period is described in the Revelation, chapters 6–19. As you know these chapters describe three series of judgments unfolding successively: the seals, the trumpets and the vials; each succeeding judgment increasing in severity. Of what do these seals, trumpets, vials—twenty-one in number—consist?

Let me swiftly summarize the events. The period begins with the taking away of the church and the removal of all divine restraint upon man. Already in the Apostle's time, there was a working of iniquity and lawlessness. The mystery of iniquity doth already work, but there is one that hindereth (II Thes. 2). There is restraint, divinely interposed.[5]

(*continued on page 131*)

6 | Scofield, like Blackstone, sees the imminent outbreak of World War I as a looming shadow portending the end times.

7 | International warfare is followed by a disintegration of law and order in society, and from there it gets worse.

8 | Again, like Blackstone, Scofield sees the Jews—albeit converted to Christianity—as having a role to play in these events, including their return to the Promised Land.

9 | Perhaps an unexpected result of Satan arriving on the scene.

Instantly, when the restraint is removed, there is universal war (Rev. 6:1–4). If you were to ask me what I think hinders, strangely and mysteriously, the breaking out of the awful war which Europe has been expecting for the past seven years, the armies there ever growing larger, coming more and more into perfect training and perfect equipment, the very sovereigns, themselves, not knowing why the war does not break out, I would say that I believe God is restraining the war until He is ready to take His own out of the world.[6] However that may be, the first thing that transpires after the church is taken away is the breaking out of universal war, and then "peace is taken from the earth," so that any man who has a private grudge against another man kills him....[7]

What follows the war is famine; following that, pestilence, then anarchy.

In the midst of "this beginning of sorrows," as Christ calls it in the 24th chapter of Matthew, a vast number of Jews turn to Jesus as their Messiah. That is the key to all that follows. From that moment, God's eye is upon those suffering Jews who have turned to Him and are receiving Jesus, though unseen yet, as their Messiah. He was rejected away back yonder by their fathers, but now in the awful trouble that has come upon the earth, they turn to Him. These believing Jews are the "brethren" of Matt. 25:40....[8]

Then follow the series of events called the trumpet judgments.... Now the Divine wrath is manifested and the distress and anguish become unspeakable (Rev. 8:9). It would be impossible to pack into words symbols of more intense woe and of more absolute anguish than are used in connection with the trumpets and vials. Through it all a world-wide preaching is carried on, mainly by the Jews....

Just here, according to Revelation 12:10–12, Satan, himself, appears upon the scene, having great wrath, because he knows his time is short. The first effect of his appearance is singular: instantly there is order. There is a sudden transformation from turbulence, disorder and anarchy to settled government once more.[9] There is instantly a

10 But this order soon turns to utter tyranny, blasphemy, and finally slaughter.

11 At the peak of this reign of terror, Christ reappears, saves his people, casts his enemies into the lake of fire, and begins his thousand-year reign upon the earth.

reconstruction of civil order over the whole prophetic earth under a monarchial form, ten confederated kings selecting or choosing one of their number as the supreme king or emperor, with his capital at Rome. Then we have the revived Roman Empire.

If we turn now in Revelation 13, we find two beasts mentioned—the beast out of the sea, and the beast out of the earth. The first is the head of civil power: the other the head of ecclesiastical power. After this—the inevitable reaction from anarchy—follows the most absolute despotism over the whole earth—ecclesiastical tyranny, civil tyranny—and the civil head of it all demanding to be worshipped as God![10]

In the meantime the disjecta membra of apostate Christendom have gathered into a confederacy which is nominally Christian, but which God calls "Babylon"—Babel meaning "confusion"—a greater parliament of religions. And now comes the last great tragedy. The civil power, the restored Roman Empire in its final ten-kingdom form, turns at last upon "Babylon," the intolerable mass of mock-religious worldliness and corruption, and utterly destroys it.

The beast out of the sea (the emperor-despot), the beast out of the earth (the "Anti-Christ," "man of sin," "false prophet"), left alone, turns savagely upon Israel. Jerusalem is once more beleaguered in utter extremity when Messiah appears in power and great glory with saints and angels.[11] He delivers His ancient people, casts the beast and false prophet alive into the lake of fire, chains Satan for one thousand years, holds the great assize of living nations (Matt. 24:31–46), judging them according to their treatment of Israel in all her long wanderings, and sets up His millennial kingdom....

Such, swiftly and most inadequately generalized, is the "great tribulation." As the next and nearest of the great prophetic periods—possibly so near that the larger part of the present population of the earth will perish in its unspeakable and indescribable horrors—it should claim from all of you immediate and most serious consideration.

May the Spirit of God help you to accept Christ now.

◆ William Stuart McBirnie (1890–1967) was an Irish evangelist who emigrated to North America and often worked as a traveling sales- man. He became a Baptist minister, pastoring churches in the Mid- west, Texas, and California. He often preached and wrote booklets on Bible prophecy during the troubled times of the Great Depression and World War II.

He has been confused with his better-known son of the same name, a preacher, pastor, prophecy speaker, anticommunist agitator, author, and successful radio and television speaker. The younger McBirnie also became president of the California Graduate School of Theology.

12 Probably the best-known feature of the biblical description of the end times is the mystical number 666. Variously identified as the mark of the beast, a clue to identifying the Antichrist, and even as the cipher of Satan himself, the meaning of this number has been the source of endless speculation.

13 McBirnie believes that the number 666 can identify someone in Rome as the Antichrist.

William S. McBirnie

from *Mussolini—Pope—"666"*

BIBLICAL NUMERICS

Scripture:

"Here is wisdom. Let he that hath understanding count the number of the beast, for it is the number of a man and his number is 666" (Rev. 13:18)....**12**

... Our text says we are to "count" and watch, if we have the wisdom, for a number which is 666.

Now what is God's number? All through the Bible we are told that God's number is seven. Why? Because God is complete and seven is the heavenly complete number. Is not Jesus Christ also complete? And the Holy Ghost? For they are three persons, one substance. Therefore if one is complete, all three must be complete. Therefore they would each have the complete number seven. Making the Divine number 777....

Now Satan dare not take God's number so he takes man's number, "6." But he, like God, has a trinity. So his trinity has for its number, Satan 6, Anti-Christ 6, and False Prophet 6. Making it man's number for the Satanic trinity, 666.

But Rev. 13:1 tells us that this will be blasphemy on somebody's head in Rome.

Rev. 13:17 tells us it is the number of his name.**13**

If you will take a close look at the mitre or crown which is worn by the Pope-elect of Rome for the induction ceremony, you will see written there, "Vicarius Filii Dei," which is the Latin for "the substitute" for the Son of God.

Is this blasphemy? Is he the substitute for the Son of God? Why is it not mentioned in the Bible? Why do we have to have a substitute? ... Christ says there is none other Name given under heaven whereby men must be saved. The Pope says (this is reported in the records of the laws enacted by the Popes in the 15th century), "When I speak it is

◆ McBirnie's use of Roman numerals to calculate the number 666 is a flexible strategy with a long history.

◆ At least one critic has pointed out that with a liberal use of Latin words standing in for a person's name, title, epithets, or related phrases (such a *vicarius filii dei* here), a determined person can use this method to associate nearly anybody with the number 666.

Christ that is speaking. When I forgive your sins, it is Christ forgiving your sins."...

Is not all this blasphemy? Is not this the type of a man who is after the working of Satan, who is a liar, saying that he is the substitute for the Son of God: Is not this blasphemy? And is it not written on his head, "VICARIUS FILII DEI"?

But one would say, "How does that spell 666"?

Back in that day they did not use numbers as we have today. So they chose letters of their Alphabet. Each letter in the Hebrew Alphabet has a numerical value. Each letter in the Greek Alphabet has a numerical value. But this is not true in the Latin. Simply six letters were chosen, as follows:

D, C, L, X, V, I (there is no U in Latin. U and V have the same numerical value). All the other letters were given zero in value, so that it would be zero, et cetera. Now look at the three words letter by letter:

V	5
I	1
C	100
A	0
R	0
I	1
U	5
S	0
	112
F	0
I	1
L	50
I	1
I	1
	53

(continued on page 139)

14 McBirnie will now use the same method to identify the Antichrist's associate, the false prophet.

15 The letters spell "VV Il Duce," where "VV" is an abbreviated form of "Viva." This is shorthand for "Viva Il Duce," the phrase with which Italians hailed Mussolini. This roundabout way of identifying Mussolini with the number 666 is typical of the circuitous and often strained mathematical methods by which various political and religious leaders have similarly been linked to this infamous number.

```
D . . . . . . . . . . . . . . . . . . . . . . . . . . . . . . . . . . .  500
E . . . . . . . . . . . . . . . . . . . . . . . . . . . . . . . . . .    0
I . . . . . . . . . . . . . . . . . . . . . . . . . . . . . . . . . .    1
                                                                     ____
                                                                      501
```

("U" and "V" have the same numerical value)   501
                                               53
                                               112
                                               ____

                    Total. 666

Meaning: "Vicarius Filii Dei"—THE SUBSTITUTE FOR THE SON OF GOD....

Turning now to "the number of his name" (Rev. 13:17), and remembering that the False Prophet is to be associated with the Anti-Christ in Rome and having seen that the blasphemy—666—is on the forehead of the Pope, therefore we are justified in counting the number of the name of the man with whom he is associated at the present time....[14]

... I say we are justified because of Mussolini's association and indicative characteristics in looking at and counting his name.

What is Mussolini's official signature that is placed on all official documents, public notices, et cetera?[15]

```
V . . . . . . . . . . . . . . . . . . . . . . . . . . . . . . . . . . .    5
V . . . . . . . . . . . . . . . . . . . . . . . . . . . . . . . . . . .    5
I . . . . . . . . . . . . . . . . . . . . . . . . . . . . . . . . . . .    1
L . . . . . . . . . . . . . . . . . . . . . . . . . . . . . . . . . . .   50
D . . . . . . . . . . . . . . . . . . . . . . . . . . . . . . . . . . .  500
V . . . . . . . . . . . . . . . . . . . . . . . . . . . . . . . . . . .    5
C . . . . . . . . . . . . . . . . . . . . . . . . . . . . . . . . . . .  100
E . . . . . . . . . . . . . . . . . . . . . . . . . . . . . . . . . . .    0
                                                                      ____
Total  . . . . . . . . . . . . . . . . . . . . . . . . . . .  666
```

16 Having established the identity of both the Antichrist and the false prophet, McBirnie now lists presumed fulfillments of other various biblical prophecies as confirmation that the end times had arrived.

17 An intriguing assertion that McBirnie does not explain.

18 In their zeal to see definite signs of the end in their own day, some interpreters have been known to become overenthusiastic.

19 Like natural disasters, wars and rumors of wars are often seen as signs of the end.

These two men are in our presence.[16]

The Jew is revived.

There is no "hire for man or beast."

There are signs in the heavens.

Ethiopia has fallen.

Mussolini is "pushing south and east."

Europe is fast preparing for the Great War between the three nations of the north and the ten of the south under the leadership of the Anti-Christ.

The "falling away" in the church is here.

There are five "christs" at the present time.[17]

We are averaging twenty-five earthquakes every twenty-four hours now. This has never been known in the history of the world.

"Power was given unto him that sat on the red horse to take the peace from the earth." There is no peace.

We have the pestilences.

The chinch bug, the screw worm, a new kind of flea, the cut worm, the hook worm, the Amazon beetle, the California worm, the black widow spider, the grasshopper, the drouth, a large number of people being injured by dogs, cats, horses. Hardly a day goes by that someone has not been scratched viciously in the face by a cat.[18]

All these are the beginning of sorrows.

We have the wars and rumors of wars, nation rising against nation, kingdom against kingdom.[19]

Luke warns us, "And when these things BEGIN to come to pass then look up and rejoice (if you are a Christian, but if you are not,—?) for your redemption draweth nigh."...

But what about the poor fellows left behind? May God continue to have mercy on them, now for Christ's sake. Amen.

◆ Christabel Pankhurst (1880–1958) was best known for her activities in Britain to secure voting rights for women. She had enthusiastically supported World War I and was a candidate for Parliament in the first election following the adoption of women's suffrage, but her failure to win the election, combined with the growing disillusionment surrounding women's suffrage, led her to look for another outlet for her seemingly inexhaustible personal energy. Toward the end of the war she happened to find a volume dealing with biblical prophecy at a bookstore, and in it she discovered the doctrine of the second coming of Christ. It became a consuming vision, the ultimate and only answer to the problems of the day, and the gateway to a new age. She could put human striving into a heavenly perspective by setting forth the promise of the reign of the Son of God on earth.

20 Europe had just experienced catastrophic destruction and suffering of truly biblical proportions. Small wonder Pankhurst saw this as a "certain" sign.

21 This same sentiment finds fresh expression with every new generation of prophecy-minded Bible interpreters.

Christabel Pankhurst

from *The Lord Cometh, The World Crisis Explained*

There has been in the past a difference of opinion among Christians as to whether the Lord Jesus Christ would make His promised second visible appearance to mankind at the beginning, or at the end of the Millennium, but in the new light cast by the remarkable world-developments that have arisen since 1914, it is now unmistakably certain that He will come to initiate the Millennium.[20] Therefore His coming is not removed from this day by a thousand years, but will occur before the new thousand-year Age begins.

The Signs of the Times are witnessing irresistibly to the truth that He is coming, and coming soon. It is awe-inspiring to watch current history fitting into the very mould of prophecy. Once you have the clue to the meaning of the existing world crisis you marvel that everybody else does not also see how prophecy is fulfilling itself in the world-events of the passing days.[21]

from *Seeing the Future*

CHAPTER XII
SIGNS OF THE TIMES: UPHEAVALS OF NATURE

Nature's violence in these latter days is no surprise to those guided by prophecy. Ever since 1917, thousands of us have known that many earthquakes and great storms were imminent. As the chord waked by the conductor's beat, the Balfour Declaration on Palestine and the Jews decisively opened the last movement of the strange symphony of this Age. The other signs were bound to follow, and nature's stressful notes were certain to be heard, as the final phase of the age, analogous by its unrest and cacophony to some modernist music, hastens to its close.

Nature's disturbance has gone crescendo, especially since the end of 1925. "Great upheavals and shocks of Nature have characterized 1926," was the verdict of one London newspaper, but the next year was

◆   Pankhurst's generation was the first to have access to a fine new invention: the radio. The rapid dissemination of news the radio made possible undoubtedly gave the sensational impression that natural disasters the world over were increasing in number and intensity.

22   Pankhurst insisted that the Zionist plan for resettling Jews in the Holy Land was one of the signs that was now heralding the end of the age. In 1925 she told a New York audience that the return of the Jews to Palestine was the supremely important factor in world affairs because it was the decisive, practical guarantee that the Son of God was soon to appear.

to see still more and greater shocks and upheavals. Floods were one scourge of 1927—the Mississippi floods, floods in New England, in European lands, floods in China. Hurricane, typhoon, and tornado raged in 1927, especially in Florida, the Bermudas, and Japan, while even the British Isles, usually spared such ordeals, experienced hurricane weather, especially in Glasgow and Lancashire.

"Great earthquakes will there be in divers places"—this sign of the age—and increased remarkably in 1927. Earthquakes occurred in Persia, in India, in America, in Crimea, in Crete, Italy, Portugal, Switzerland, in France, in Southern Germany, in California, in Australia, in China with 100,000 deaths and great towns overwhelmed, in Siberia, in Alaska, in Palestine, and in the British Isles. So rarely are British earthquakes felt, that the perceptible shaking of twenty counties and the Channel Isles was significant....

"Great signs shall there be from heaven," so goes the prediction—and some time since this sign appeared faintly and incipiently. Reports such as this were made: "Meteor 600 feet in length, like a gigantic, blazing skyrocket passes over city" ... "Large and blazing meteorite outshines the moon in brilliance" ... "A conspicuous spectacle, a large meteor, probably derived from Halley's periodical comet; curious feature was its extremely long flight from the west side of Aquarius to past Eta Virginis." Phenomena in the skies will be magnified and multiplied—but not until the general climax will they develop to the full....

CHAPTER XV
SIGNS OF THE TIMES: THE JEWS IN PALESTINE

Zionism is the sign of all signs of Messiah's coming. How wonderful it is that just as the Jews are attaining a greater influence than they have ever had in the Gentile world, there should be this turning again to Zion![22]

Zionism is a very just cause, a very great movement. The belittling jest or doubt of some Gentile critics is of no account. The writer of these pages is better qualified by experience, than some, to judge the significance and the prospects of Zionism, having been concerned in another movement, which began as a weak and small thing and eventuated in the

◆ In addition to the return of the Jews to Palestine, she saw the signs of Armageddon multiplying rapidly—wars and rumors of war, the blasphemous actions of the Soviet dictators, the arrogance of science, the decay of faith and moral standards, and the worship of money and pleasure.

Over the next years she continued to identify current events—the onset of the depression, catastrophic unemployment, an earthquake in England, and new discoveries in science—as signs of the imminent return of Christ. She said the Bible was the one sure guide to world affairs. She predicted a victory for Franco in the Spanish civil war, since Spain was destined to be part of the Roman Empire that Mussolini and Hitler were reviving. In fact, she even developed a friendship with Winston Churchill. He shared her pessimistic view of historical development and was fascinated by her idea that the great power blocs of the world would clash in the struggle to determine who would emerge as the true and ultimate Antichrist, the one who would challenge God himself and provoke the battle of Armageddon.

enfranchisement of millions of women who, from being politically non-existent, became numerically predominant, with a corresponding change in their whole social influence. As great a transformation in human institutions as the world has ever known! Zionism, to an eye thus trained in the school of practical experience, has, and had from the beginning, all the mark and promise of a practical success.

The Zionist pioneer, Herzl, spoke the sheer truth when in 1897, on the conclusion of the first Zionist Congress, he said: "I have founded the Jewish State." That year, 1897, marked the starting point of modern Zionism: the idea took root in the Jewish mind. Twenty years later, in 1917, the phase of realization began. Just in the same way women's enfranchisement in Great Britain, now a great accomplished fact, was an idea in a few minds for twice as long, forty years and more, before the phase of realization began in the first decade of the present century, and ended in victory in the second decade. Modern Zionism has followed a like course. One well remembers the day when, from women themselves, the idea of voting, because unfamiliar, met with indifference, and even, where some were concerned, resistance. They were accustomed to being voteless: why not, thought many of them, leave things alone, especially as success was in their view doubtful, and even if realized might mean the loss of some existing privilege. Exactly the same indifference, and even greater resistance, have many Jews shown toward Zionism. Exactly in the same way will their indifference and resistance be overcome. A conquering idea is the return to Zion! Moreover, the Zionist pioneers of the first hour, and those of today, are imbued with the spirit and purpose that win! Those who have themselves been something of pioneers....

Since 1917, the door to success has been wide open, but even before Turkey plunged into the Great War, before the British campaign in Palestine, before the taking of Jerusalem, and then of all Palestine, it was enough to see Zionism at work among American Jewry, the strongest in the world as to numbers and wealth, to know that success must come. In that campaign, doubt and opposition were destined to go under, because in spite of everything, Zionism has an ally in every Jewish heart, and

23 Pankhurst singles out the vital role of women for Zionist success. It is interesting to notice that she was warmly received by the fundamentalist audiences to whom she spoke. She toured Canada and North America several times and was a great success among the various audiences who would have normally rejected a woman preacher. This can probably be accounted for by the evangelical penchant for lionizing important converts to the faith. In more contemporary times, sports, entertainment, and even criminal celebrities such as White House counsel-turned Watergate criminal-turned high-profile Christian Charles Colson fill this same role.

◆ An Australian evangelical preacher, Leonard Sale-Harrison (1875–1956) held prophetic conferences at churches in Britain and North America, especially during the 1920s and 1930s, and published more than a dozen books and pamphlets. He saw signs of the end times in, among other things, contemporary economic, political, and scientific developments. His books went through several editions and were updated in light of current events, selling tens of thousands of copies. Sale-Harrison captivated the public of his day, much like the popular prophecy teacher Hal Lindsey captured the American public's imagination in the 1970s.

24 One chilling sign of the coming of the Antichrist was the founding of British Monomarks, Ltd., a company that would provide customers with an identity mark that could be used in commerce. This was the mark of the beast described in Revelation 13:16–18.

because the Zionists are charged with a conquering zeal and inspiration—and not least the Deborahs among them. Indeed, it was the Deborahs who, in a chance and slight glimpse of the movement, were, to an outside observer, the decisive sign and demonstration of its immense potentiality. The part of women, in a national revival, in stimulating and sustaining enthusiasm and hope, can be, evidently, most important.[23]

Dr. Leonard Sale-Harrison

from *The Resurrection of the Old Roman Empire, The League of Nations and the Future of Europe*

SIGNS OF APPROACHING TROUBLE

The writer called to inquire at the office of the Monomarks, Ltd., which extends its ramifications throughout Europe. It is named in England "The British Monomarks, Ltd.," and its London offices are at 97 High Holborn, London. As a Company it is conducted on correct business lines, and its motives are entirely honourable. We have nothing to say against their sincerity and integrity, though we do feel that their system will lead to far-reaching results that they do not, perhaps cannot, anticipate.[24]

The service it offers the general public applies to—(1) The restoration of lost property. (2) It gives a free letter forwarding service. (3) A free box number. (4) An emergency telegraphic address. (5) A perfect nom-de-plume—which through Monomarks, Ltd., serves both as your name and postal address. (6) It enables subscribers to obtain reduction of premium for all insurance risks on portable property, etc., etc., etc. The Monomark consists of three or more numbers or characters, and costs each annual subscriber the modest sum of five shillings ($1.25). Life subscriptions are from four guineas ($21.00). The fee being so exceedingly moderate ensures its universal adoption wherever the "Monomark's" service operates. The advantages of the system are set out in a pamphlet which states 20 reasons why "your Monomark is more efficient than your initials"—the first being that "it gives you an unmistakable identity amongst other people of the same name."

25 This perfectly reasonable and ingenious business proposition takes on frighteningly nefarious undertones when viewed in the light of Revelation's cryptic prophecy.

26 Sale-Harrison matched scriptures with events in the life and times of Benito Mussolini. He based his interpretation on the image in King Nebuchadnezzar's dream (Dan. 2), which had feet of clay and iron. He believed this described the Roman Empire in the last days. The clay represented extremely democratic elements, such as the socialists, while the iron depicted the strong body of men who would stand and support law and order. The latter group, identified with the Fascists, would call for a superman or strong ruler (Antichrist) to bring order out of chaos. Mussolini, who may or may not have been the final Antichrist, was certainly preparing the way for him.

He then explained how the Italian dictator, in conformity with biblical prophecy, was reviving the Roman Empire. His territorial conquests were designed at converting the Mediterranean Sea into an Italian lake, like the *mare nostrum* of ancient Rome. The Duce was even trying to establish a state cult with himself at the center. Like the Caesars, he took control of all the major offices of state and restored the ancient buildings of the city of Rome. He even planned to erect a huge statue in his own honor, thus fulfilling Revelation 13:14–15.

This information shows how the world is quietly but quickly preparing for the manifestation of the Man of Sin, and subtly making use of everyday affairs, legitimate enough in themselves.[25]

The Monomarks, Ltd. is becoming a universal trading concern. Wherever this has been established it is rapidly increasing the desire to own a private monomark. The advance of the use of the monomarks is but the beginning of the fulfillment of that terrible prophecy which is given to us in Revelation 13:16–18.

"He causeth all, both small and great, rich and poor, free and bond, to receive a mark in their right hand, or on their foreheads: And that no man might buy or sell, save he that had the mark, or the name of the beast, or the number of his name. Here is wisdom. Let him that hath understanding count the number of the beast: for it is the number of a man; and his number six hundred, threescore and six."

How near must we be to the period referred to in these verses?

AMERICA'S INVESTIGATIONS

Fascism has been very active in Mexico, Central and South America, which has been causing concern to the Administration at Washington, D.C. Mussolini declares that those of Italian blood must be controlled by his commands....[26]

Mussolini is determined not to lose his nationals by allowing them to become citizens of another country. "My order," he says, "is that an Italian citizen must remain an Italian citizen, no matter in what land he lives, even to the seventh generation."

He hopes thereby to add half a million soldiers to his side when the Empire is called to arms. There are therefore well-organized triumvirates which rule over local Fascios (branches) throughout certain countries. The plans carried out are intricate and work with remarkable precision. We point this out to show how wonderfully the Resurrection of the Old Roman Empire is being formed, as it is outlined in the Word of God.

27 Further fulfillments of prophecy were also found in the advance of science through such things as robotics, television, and the first world-wide radio broadcast by the pope in 1931, which Sale-Harrison viewed as a sinister expansion of papal power.

The World Radio of April, 1929, stated the remarkable fact that the wave lengths for both Moscow and Rome were 666; at least, this is very interesting and significant.

THE ADVANCE OF SCIENCE

Advance in science is so marked in these days that one wonders what achievement will be accomplished next. The most startling of recent developments is the "Robot." It is a mechanical man worked by electricity. It is most weird and uncanny. It can answer certain questions put to it in a way that inspires awe, and can do other remarkable things.[27]

Sound can be sent on a beam of light, while dual television and radio tests have been successfully made in England. In America science has so advanced that invisible rays can be made to operate miles away, and some of the experiments have shown almost uncanny results....

February 12, 1931, will be remembered as a unique preparation for the fulfillment of Revelation 13 and 17. The radio address by Pope Pius IX from HVJ—the radio station of "The State of Vatican City"—was received with superstitious awe and reverence by the Roman Catholic faithful the world over. It was quite understood that such a speech would not fail to appeal for a universal acceptance of the Roman Catholic faith. It cannot be ignored that this performance is of deep significance for it is the first time that a Pope has sent out a worldwide message which has been received simultaneously by the whole of his flock. It is the beginning of an asserted authority, which makes his sway more marvelously powerful than ever could have been conceived by man. When the time arrives the Pope will be able to issue decrees and instructions which will have simultaneous acceptance amongst the Catholic communities of the world. Regular programs are not to be given from this station. Though this event is used as a means of great Roman Catholic propaganda, yet its significance is very far-reaching. All this is preparing for the carrying out of many things prophesied in Revelation 13 and 17.

Many have wondered how Revelation 13:12 could be fulfilled. With the advance of modern science this is not difficult to understand.

◆ A Baptist preacher and author, Clarence Larkin (1850–1924) graduated with a degree in mechanical engineering from the Polytechnic College of Philadelphia. After he became a dispensational premillennialist he began making charts for his pulpit ministry. These were so popular that he sold them along with his commentaries on Revelation, Daniel, and numerous other parts of the Bible. In the days before audio-visual tools, this technology was widely used in public presentations to illustrate some of the intricacies of dispensational doctrine.

The chart reproduced here represents in concise visual fashion the principle that although the prophets clearly beheld and accurately foretold future events, their particular perspective was nonetheless not a comprehensive one. They could not see everything. From "Our View-Point"—the experience of subsequent history and a new method of synthesizing different portions of scripture—we are able to see much more.

Such a diagram nicely dispels any vexing doubts the believer may have due to the long delay of Christ's return. The gap between Daniel's sixty-ninth and seventieth weeks—"The Valley of the Church"—can stretch indefinitely without compromising either the prophets' divine inspiration or the dispensationalist timeline.

CHART Nº 2

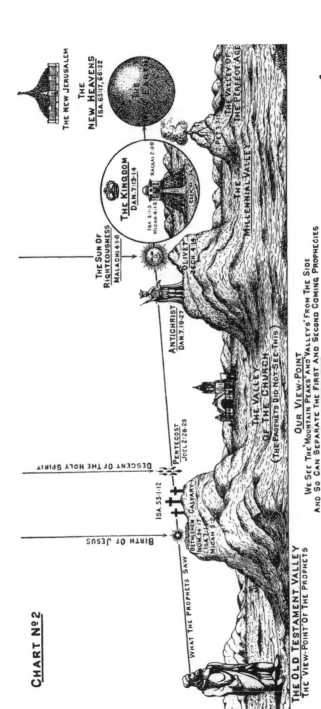

THE NEW JERUSALEM

THE **NEW HEAVENS**
ISA.65:17, 66:22

THE EARTH

THE **KINGDOM**
DAN.7:13-14

HAGGAI 2:5-9

EZEK.37:26

ISA. 2:1-3
MICAH 4:1-2

THE VALLEY OF
THE PERFECT AGE
2 PET.3:13

THE SUN OF
RIGHTEOUSNESS
MALACHI 4:1-6

THE
MILLENNIAL VALLEY

OLIVET
2 CH. 4:14

ANTICHRIST
DAN.7:19-27

PENTECOST
JOEL 2:28-29

DESCENT OF THE HOLY SPIRIT

ISA. 53:1-12

CALVARY

BETHLEHEM
NUM.24:17
(ISA.7:14)
MICAH 5:2

THE VALLEY
OF THE CHURCH
(THE PROPHETS DID NOT SEE THIS)

BIRTH OF JESUS

WHAT THE PROPHETS SAW

THE OLD TESTAMENT VALLEY
THE VIEW-POINT OF THE PROPHETS

OUR VIEW-POINT
WE SEE THE "MOUNTAIN PEAKS" AND "VALLEYS" FROM THE SIDE
AND SO CAN SEPARATE THE FIRST AND SECOND COMING PROPHECIES

THE "MOUNTAIN PEAKS" OF PROPHECY

DESIGNED AND DRAWN BY
GLARENCE LARKIN,
FOXCHASE, PHILA., PA.
COPYRIGHTED

◆ During the last half of the twentieth century, dispensationalism began to enter the mainstream of American life. Its combination of pessimism and optimism seemed especially suited to the times. Three major developments of the post–World War II era encouraged this. The first was the development of atomic weapons with incomprehensible destructive power and delivery systems that leave no place on earth safe from the threat of thermonuclear annihilation. The second was the establishment of the Jewish State of Israel in 1948 and the successful defense of its territory in later conflicts with its neighbors. The third was the emergence of the Cold War, the silent conflict between the United States and the Soviet Union. Conservative Christian circles in particular saw the Cold War as an ideological struggle between democracy and dictatorship, freedom and slavery. It was more than just a geopolitical conflict for leadership in those areas of the world regarded by the two major powers as their spheres of interest.

These themes pervade the prophetic and apocalyptic literature that rolled off conservative presses. Although there are many examples of sensationalist prophetic teachers, perhaps the most famous in the last half of the twentieth century is Hal Lindsey. Assisted by freelance writer Carole C. Carlson, he published his seminal book in 1970 with the intriguing title *The Late Great Planet Earth*.

This was dispensational premillennialism dressed up for the modern age. It soon became the best-selling nonfiction book of the 1970s, according to the *New York Times*, and was translated into more than fifty languages with sales in excess of thirty-five million copies. A film version of the book was produced in 1978, with narration by Orson Welles, Hal Lindsey, and others.

1 A factor in Lindsey's widespread popularity is his fervent insistence that the biblical prophets of old were speaking direct and dire warnings in "clear and unmistakable prophetic signs" about events in our very own lifetime.

2 Lindsey could easily be describing the Larkin diagram reproduced on page 155.

9 □ Into the Twenty-first Century

Hal Lindsey

from *The Late Great Planet Earth*

In this book I am attempting to step aside and let the prophets speak.[1]

However, compared to the speculation of most that is called prophetic today, the Bible contains clear and unmistakable prophetic signs. We are able to see right now in this Best Seller predictions made centuries ago being fulfilled right before our eyes.

Two completely different portraits of a coming Messiah were described by the Old Testament prophets [one of a suffering servant, another of a conquering king]....

For those who lived prior to the birth of Jesus of Nazareth, the perspective of these two portraits of the Messiah was difficult to understand.

Imagine a man looking at a range of mountains. He is able to see the peak of one mountain, and beyond it the peak of another. However, from this vantage point, he cannot see the valley which separates these two mountains.

Men viewed the two portraits of the Messiah in the same manner. They saw two different persons, but missed the connection. They did not perceive that there could be just one Messiah, coming in two different roles, and separated by the valley of time.[2]

◆ Basic to Lindsey's eschatology is his identification of various "signs" that are the pieces of the jigsaw-like "prophecy puzzle" that "can be pieced together to make a coherent picture, even though the pieces are scattered in small bits throughout the Old and New Testaments."

3 One of the key pieces in this puzzle is the creation of the Jewish State of Israel in 1948. He stops short of actually announcing a specific date, but Lindsey here insinuates that Christ's return will likely occur in or around 1988.

4 The sequence of events that will occur during the tribulation are those that many dispensationalist prophecy preachers tend to identify. Among them is the appearance of the Antichrist, who will head up a revived Roman Empire composed of the European Community. He will encourage the revival of the dark occult practices of ancient Babylon, which will accompany the growth of apostasy of Christian churches from historic Christianity.

Jesus said that this [sign] would indicate that He was "at the door," ready to return. Then He said, "Truly I say to you, *this generation* will not pass away until all these things take place" (Matthew 24:34 NASB).

What generation? Obviously, in context, the generation that would see the signs—chief among them the rebirth of Israel. A generation in the Bible is something like forty years. If this is a correct deduction, then within forty years or so of 1948, all these things could take place. Many scholars who have studied Bible prophecy all their lives believe that this is so.[3]

The time is ripe and getting riper for the Great Dictator, the one we call the "Future Fuehrer." This is the one who is predicted in the Scriptures very clearly and called the "Antichrist."...

All around the world today the increase in the mystic, occult, and even devil-worship is so pronounced that people are beginning to question what it's all about. There are churches in some of the major cities of America which actually incorporate into their "religious ceremonies" the worship of the devil....

However, the Satan-worship which will be initiated at the time of the world reign of the Future Fuehrer will make today's antics of the cultists look like nursery school.[4]

5   Lindsey displays a fascination with current events and identifies other signs of the rapidly approaching tribulation in the geopolitical maneuverings of the world's great powers. This includes the ominous presence of the atheistic Soviet Union, which, due to geography and various political developments, Lindsey believed to be the great northern confederacy that would sweep down upon Israel. Similarly, he identified an Arab-African alliance as Daniel's king of the south and "Red China" as Revelation's king of the east, the mighty power that could field untold millions of soldiers and attack Israel from across the Euphrates River. Lindsey goes so far as to chart troop movements on maps of the likely route of the "Russian amphibious assault" on Israel and speculates at length about other military strategies and battlefield tactics.

The decline and fall of Communism presented Lindsey and many other apocalyptic interpreters with a problem. Almost without exception they had identified Russia with Gog and Magog, and especially the "Rosh" mentioned in Ezekiel 38:2–3. They also associated the place-name *Meshech* in the passage with Moscow. The collapse of the Soviet Union has such interpreters searching for a new entity which fits their understanding of prophecy.

Associating the Soviet Union with the monolithic fountainhead of all wickedness in the world allowed these interpreters to view America as the land of virtue. The prophecy preachers' use of Daniel and Revelation compelled believers to think in terms of a grand end-times drama, with the United States engaged in a struggle with an evil Communist empire.

6   Lindsey claims that John's words show "precisely" what is going to happen, yet quickly concedes that the imagery can be "difficult" to understand.

This kind of rhetoric is central to Lindsey's writing. Rejecting modern critical methods of studying the Bible, he urges readers not to believe scholars who explain away the clear and evident meaning of a given text, yet he uses his own "special insight" to mold the biblical materials into his own interpretive scheme.

The final evidence for identifying this northern commander lies in its geographical location from Israel.

Ezekiel puts great stress on this by saying three times that this great enemy of Israel would come from their "uttermost north."...

You need only to take a globe to verify this exact geographical fix. There is only one nation to the "uttermost north" of Israel—the U.S.S.R.[5]

In the twenty odd years since the fall of China to the Communists there has been a steady relentless preparation for all-out war with the free world. Though the living conditions of the eight hundred million or more people of Red China are still basically like the nineteenth century, they have made remarkable progress in the production of weapons for war....

... We live at a time in history when it is no longer incredible to think of the Orient with an army of 200 million soldiers. In fact, a recent television documentary on Red China ... quoted the boast of the Chinese themselves that they could field a "people's army" of 200 million militiamen. In their own boast they named the same number as the Biblical prediction. Coincidence?

In Revelation 17 the apostle John has a vision which shows the future and precisely what is going to happen on earth the last seven years before Christ returns....

Look what John says in Revelation 17:3–5: "And he carried me away in the Spirit into a wilderness; and I saw a woman sitting on a scarlet beast, full of blasphemous names, having seven heads and ten horns.... [And the woman held] in her hand a cup full of abominations and of the unclean things of her immorality, and upon her forehead a name was written, a mystery, 'BABYLON THE GREAT, THE MOTHER OF HARLOTS AND THE ABOMINATIONS OF THE EARTH'" (NASB).

It is sometimes difficult for the Bible reader to grasp this symbolism.[6]

◆ This tendency is even more evident is his book *Apocalypse Code* (1997), based upon the book of Revelation. He portrays the writer of Revelation as "an 'eyewitness' to events of the twentieth and twenty-first centuries." John was a "first-century time traveler" who was translated to the beginning of the twenty-first century and vividly shown a global war fought with modern weapons. As Lindsey puts it, John "testified and God bore witness" that he actually saw and heard things like supersonic jet aircraft, attack helicopters, modern battle tanks, intercontinental ballistic missiles, nuclear submarines, even space stations and satellites.

Lindsey says that John was then brought back to the first century and told to write an account of this future time. He was to do this in "encoded symbols." And now the time has come for these prophecies to be "uncoded," which requires the interpretation of "a Christian [who is] guided by the spirit of God." The need for such interpretation would seem to be at odds with his oft-repeated claim that he is letting the prophets speak for themselves.

7 This common premillennialist teaching posits that anyone with an alternative understanding of the role and meaning of biblical prophecy are by definition apostate—and therefore further evidence that we are in the end times.

8 Lindsey follows in the footsteps of Dwight L. Moody and countless others in using the imminent return of Christ as a goad to spur readers into considering their own spiritual condition.

◆ In the beginning, Lindsey's books sold not because he was famous or because of the literary quality of his work. Rather, they sold because they met the needs of a great number of people. It is also interesting material. By aligning his interpretation with today's news, he makes the Bible a contemporary document for his readers. No marketing ploy is missed in his cliché-ridden application of scripture to contemporary events. Earthquakes, El Niño, AIDS, UFOs, and Y2K are all included in his prophetic detail. Thus, his readers can master the true meaning behind the news and even get a glimpse of what is coming in the "new world tomorrow."

We need to be alert. When we hear church leaders, teachers, or preachers questioning the visible return of Christ, this is a doctrine of apostasy.[7]

As the battle of Armageddon reaches its awful climax and it appears that all life will be destroyed on earth—in this very moment Jesus Christ will return to save man from self-extinction.

As history races toward this moment, are you afraid or looking with hope for deliverance? The answer should reveal to you your spiritual condition.

One way or another history continues in a certain acceleration toward the return of Christ. Are you ready?[8]

◆ Tim LaHaye became well known in conservative religious circles for several reasons, in addition to his numerous apocalyptic publications. He was involved in the founding of the Institute for Creation Research, an organization for the distribution of antievolutionary materials, and he joined the movement in the search for Noah's ark on Mount Ararat. But his major claim to fame was a book titled *Spirit-Controlled Temperament* that became a best seller among conservative Christians, which fused an antiquated explanation of psychological temperaments with biblical themes. With his wife, Beverly, he wrote *The Act of Marriage: The Beauty of Sexual Love*, and together the LaHayes won national prominence by holding workshops on the family and supporting traditional gender roles. They were even named the Christian "power couple" by *Time* magazine in a cover article about the twenty-five most influential evangelicals in America.

In the early 1990s, LaHaye had the idea of writing a fictional story about the "rapture" of the church. He believed this would be helpful in winning others to Christ. After some abortive attempts, his agent suggested that he collaborate with another writer, Jerry Jenkins. This proved to be a masterstroke because Jenkins was an extremely capable writer, having been an editor for Moody Press and the author of more than a hundred Christian books, including several sports biographies. They worked out a unique method by which LaHaye would send Jenkins a 70- to 100-page scripture-based prophetic outline for each book, and then Jenkins would turn it into a fictional story that would convey the meaning in an exciting contemporary tale replete with interesting characters and relevant themes.

9 Rayford Steele, an airline pilot and one of the novel's central characters, receives the news from a flight attendant that, midflight over the Atlantic, people have vanished from the plane, leaving behind clothes, jewelry—and, of course, *them*.

10 One character e-mails Cameron "Buck" Williams, a crack reporter and another of the book's main characters, and comments on the mysterious disappearances. Lines such as this one reveal the novel's theological leanings. Children, who are not yet accountable for their actions, are "innocents" and so have been taken, whereas being a nice person is no guarantee of salvation.

Tim LaHaye and Jerry B. Jenkins

from *Left Behind*

Her knees buckled as she tried to speak, and her voice came in a whiny squeal.

"People are missing," she managed in a whisper, burying her head in his chest.

[Rayford] took her shoulders and tried to push her back, but she fought to stay close. "What do you m—?"

She was sobbing now, her body out of control. "A whole bunch of people, just gone!"

"Hattie, this is a big plane. They've wandered to the lavs or—"

She pulled his head down so she could speak directly into his ear.... "I've been everywhere. I'm telling you, dozens of people are missing."

"Hattie, it's still dark. We'll find—" ...

"Ray! Their shoes, their socks, their clothes, everything was left behind. These people are gone!"[9]

> "Have you noticed it seems to have struck only the innocents? Everyone we know who's gone is either a child or a very nice person. On the other hand, some truly wonderful people are still here."[10]

[11] Likewise, believing in God, even aligning with a particular theology, isn't enough: Despite his witnessing and believing in a bona fide miracle prior to the novel's opening, Cameron was left behind.

[12] Rayford returns home to find his wife and son—who were devout Christians—gone. Rayford quickly understands the truth of what's happened and wonders what anyone in his shoes would wonder: Is it too late for me?

[13] Rayford tracks down his wife's Bible to begin his search for answers, which he ultimately finds within its pages. By allowing a character with limited knowledge of the Bible to start his investigation from scratch, the novel provides the reader with an inviting entrée into biblical texts and apocalyptic traditions. *Left Behind* acts in much the same fashion as *The Scofield Reference Bible* did for an earlier generation: It presents the biblical texts along with accessible commentary (in this case, fiction) from a dispensational perspective.

[14] The novel never claims to be more than a fictional story, but the narrative draws unmistakably clear parallels with real-world beliefs about the Bible, prophecy, and salvation. Rayford's fictional ponderings such as these might easily inspire readers to ask such questions of their own lives in the here and now, "before it's too late."

"Come on, Cameron. You know you got your mind right when you saw what God did for Israel."

"Granted, but don't start calling me a Christian. Deist is as much as I'll cop to."

"Stay in town long enough to come to my church, and God'll getcha."

"He's already got me, Lucinda. But Jesus is another thing."[11]

Irene and Ray would not be coming back, and he didn't know if he would ever see them again, because he didn't know if there were second chances on this heaven thing.[12]

He wanted to investigate, to learn, to know, to act. He started by searching for a Bible, not the family Bible that had collected dust on his shelf for years, but Irene's. Hers would have notes in it, maybe something that could point him in the right direction.

It wasn't hard to find.... Would there be some guide? An index? Something that referred to the Rapture or the judgment or something? If not, maybe he'd start at the end. If *genesis* meant "beginning," maybe *revelation* had something to do with the end....[13]

Worst of all, he feared he was reading the Bible too late. Clearly he was too late to have gone to heaven with his wife and son. But was he too late, period?[14]

15 With the instantaneous disappearance of millions of people across the globe, civilization is thrown into immediate chaos and lingering confusion. Various characters espouse an assortment of theories on the nature of the disappearances, just as one might expect in such a situation. Here, Buck presses one man for his ideas. Yet in the world of the novel, the only satisfactory answer is that the true Christians have gone to meet the Lord in the air, as predicted by scripture.

16 Rayford tries to convince his daughter Chloe, a Stanford University student, that the disappearances were the work of God. The *Left Behind* series has attracted readers beyond dispensational circles partly because of the way many of the individuals such as Chloe voice their struggles with faith.

"So, you don't buy the kidnapping space aliens, but you connect the disappearances with UFOs?" [Buck said.]

"I'm just sayin' it's not like *E.T.*, with creatures and all that. I think our ideas of what space people would look like is way too simple and rudimentary. If there is intelligent life out there, and there has to be just because of the sheer odds—"

"What do you mean?"

"The vastness of space."

"Oh, so many stars and so much area that something has to be out there somewhere."

"Exactly.... [And if there are,] I'm thinking they're sophisticated and advanced enough that they can do things to us we've never dreamed of."

"Like making people disappear right out of their clothes."

"Sounded pretty silly until the other night, didn't it?"

Buck nodded.[15]

"Apparently those who were taken were recognized by God as truly his. How else can I say it?"

"Daddy, what does this make God? Some sick, sadistic dictator?"

"Careful, honey. You think I'm wrong, but what if I'm right?"

"Then God is spiteful, hateful, mean. Who wants to go to heaven with a God like that?"

"If that's where your mom and Raymie are, that's where I want to be."

"I want to be with them, too, Daddy! But tell me how this fits with a loving, merciful God. When I went to church, I got tired of hearing how loving God is. He never answered *my* prayers and I never felt like he knew me or cared about me. Now you're saying I was right. He didn't. I didn't qualify, so I got left behind?"[16]

17 Rayford and Chloe turn to Bruce Barnes, an erstwhile pastor who was also left behind. Bruce outlines for the Steeles—and for the reader—the importance of true repentance and salvation. Bruce's speech amounts to a evangelical gospel presentation within the fictional narrative, concluding with an invitation to receive Christ. Later, a videotape left behind by Bruce Barnes's senior pastor—who was raptured—offers a suggested prayer to "become a child of God." The plot is gripping, but the book's real-life agenda is thinly veiled.

18 Bruce's final words to the Steeles, which dramatically end the chapter, powerfully recall the concluding words from Dwight L. Moody's sermon: "Now, let the question go around, 'Am I ready to meet the Lord if He comes tonight?'"

19 These words, also from the videotape left by Bruce Barnes's senior pastor, succinctly summarize the novel's fundamental assumption that biblical prophecy is primarily concerned with foretelling the future. Readers unfamiliar with the Bible may not be aware that the biblical prophets themselves emphasized not apocalyptic forecasts but rather what they saw as God's pressing agenda in more immediate circumstances, including justice for the poor, mercy for the powerless, and guileless worship of God.

"I especially liked the parts about God being forgiving. I was a sinner, and I never changed. I just kept getting forgiveness because I thought God was bound to do that. He had to. Verses that said if we confessed our sins he was faithful and just to forgive us and to cleanse us. I knew other verses said you had to believe *and* receive, to trust and abide, but to me that was sort of theological mumbo jumbo. I wanted the bottom line, the easiest route, the simplest path....

... "[But] I had been a phony, I had set up my own brand of Christianity that may have made for a life of freedom but cost me my soul...."

... [Rayford asked,] "So, how do we become true Christians?"

"I'm going to walk you through that," Bruce said.[17]

"But let me leave you with one little reminder of urgency.... What would be worse than finally finding God and then dying without him because you waited too long?"[18]

"Bible prophecy is history written in advance."[19]

20 As the novel progresses, the characters begin to see more prophecies fulfilled when a small group of politically and financially prominent individuals, particularly the charismatic Nicolae Carpathia, rise rapidly to world leadership through the United Nations. These events convince the believers that they are indeed entering the tribulation.

By the end of the first volume, many of the main characters have received Christ and have formed an elite Tribulation Force, dedicated to stopping the evil politician Nicolae Carpathia, Secretary-General of the United Nations, whom they believe to be none other than the Antichrist himself.

◆ These readable and action-packed books popularize dispensational teaching and lead many of their readers to believe that current events are leading to the immediate rapture of children and "true" Christians.

One scholar has suggested several other characteristics of *Left Behind* and its sequels that may account for their popularity. These include the fact that evil comes from the outside and consequently leads to the comforting outlook that one side is altogether right and good and the other wrong and evil. This view that people are either all bad or all good justifies the notion that the solution to our problems is the destruction of the wicked in a final triumph of the good that leaves no ambiguity. Such a worldview enables the use of all sorts of violence and dreadful weapons to accomplish the ends of the "saints." In this same vein, it has been pointed out that the tribulation saints steal, hate, lie, smuggle, blackmail with no sense of remorse, and generally live a materialistic lifestyle at the personal level. That seems to be at odds with the separated life taught by earlier generations of dispensationalists.

[Bruce said,] "As you know, I've been studying Revelation and several commentaries about end-times events....

... "It looks to me, and to many of the experts who came before us, that this period of history we're in right now will last for seven years.... The last half of the seven years is called the Great Tribulation, and if we are alive at the end of it, we will be rewarded by seeing the Glorious Appearing of Christ."

Loretta raised her hand. "Why do you keep saying 'if we survive'? What are these judgments?"

"They get progressively worse, and if I'm reading this right, they will be harder and harder to survive.... [And] we may suffer horrible deaths. If we somehow make it through the seven terrible years, especially the last half, the Glorious Appearing will be all that more glorious. Christ will come back to set up his thousand-year reign on earth."

"The Millennium."

"Exactly.... [But] the Antichrist will soon come to power...."[20]

Notes ☐

Introduction

1. The term for a thousand is repeated five times in Revelation 20:1–6. The doctrine of the thousand-year reign of Christ is called millennialism or millenarianism from the Latin form of the word for a thousand, or chiliasm from the Greek.

2. Helpful information on millennialism is available in the following works: Robert G. Clouse, ed., *The Meaning of the Millennium: Four Views* (Downers Grove, IL: InterVarsity, 1977); Stanley J. Grenz, *The Millennial Maze: Sorting Out Evangelical Options* (Downers Grove, IL: InterVarsity Press, 1992); Theodore Olson, *Millennialism, Utopianism, and Progress* (Toronto: University of Toronto Press, 1982); C. A. Patrides and J. Wittreich, *The Apocalypse in English Renaissance Thought and Literature* (Ithaca: Cornell University Press, 1984); and Ernest L. Tuveson, *Millennium and Utopia: A Study in the Background of the Idea of Progress* (Berkeley: University of California Press, 1949).

3. For one of the more perceptive presentations of the postmillennial view, see Loraine Boettner, *The Millennium* (Philadelphia: Presbyterian and Reformed, 1966).

4. For more on amillennialism, consult Anthony A. Hoekema, *The Bible and the Future* (Grand Rapids: Eerdmans, 1979).

5. Premillennialism is explained by Clarence Bass, *Backgrounds to Dispensationalism* (Grand Rapids: Eerdmans, 1960); Charles L. Feinberg, *Millennialism: The Two Major Views* (Winona Lake, IN: BMH Books, 1985); Charles Ryrie, *Dispensationalism Today* (Chicago: Moody Press, 1965); Ernest R. Sandeen, *The Roots of Fundamentalism: British and American Millenarianism* (Chicago: University of Chicago Press, 1970); and Timothy P. Weber, *Living in the Shadow of the Second Coming: American Premillennialism, 1875–1982* (Chicago: University of Chicago Press, 1987).

6. Samuel Sewell, *Phaenomena quaedam Apocalyptica or Some Few Lines Towards a Description of the New Heavens* (Boston, 1697).

7. Further typologies of millennialism may be found in Paul Christianson, *Reformers and Babylon: English Apocalyptic Visions from the Eve of the Reformation to the Eve of the Civil War* (Toronto: University of Toronto Press, 1978); James A. DeJong, *As the Waters Cover the Sea: Millennial Expectations in the Rise*

of *Anglo-American Missions 1640–1810* (Kampen, Netherlands: Kok N. V., 1970); Katherine R. Firth, *The Apocalyptic Tradition in Reformation Britain, 1530–1645* (Oxford: Oxford University Press, 1979); James F. Maclear, "New England and the Fifth Monarchy: The Quest for the Millennium in Early American Puritanism," in *Puritan New England: Essays on Religion, Society, and Culture*, eds. A. T. Vaughan and F. J. Bremer (New York: St. Martin's, 1977), 65–89; Ian Murray, *The Puritan Hope: A Study in Revival and the Interpretation of Prophecy* (London: Banner of Truth Trust, 1971); and James West Davidson's fine book, *The Logic of Millennial Thought* (New Haven: Yale University Press, 1977).

8. Bernard McGinn, *Visions of the End, Apocalyptic Traditions in the Middle Ages* (New York: Columbia University Press, 1979).

9. Norman Cohn, *The Pursuit of the Millennium, Revolutionary and Mystical Anarchists of the Middle Ages* (New York: Oxford University Press, 1970).

10. Robin Bruce Barnes, *Prophecy and Gnosis: Apocalypticism in the Wake of the Lutheran Reformation* (Stanford: Stanford University Press, 1988).

11. Francis X. Gumerlock, "Millennialism and the Early Church Councils: Was Chiliasm Condemned at Constantinople?" in *Fides Et Historia* 2 (Summer/Fall 2004), 83–95. As Gumerlock summarizes his conclusions: "According to historical theologian, Jaroslav Pelikan, chiliast beliefs escaped official anathema by all of the early councils because they did not deny the creed. My investigation of the canons of the early councils similarly has uncovered no condemnation of chiliasm by them" (p. 94).

12. Howard Hotson, *Paradise Postponed, Johann Heinrich (Alsted) and the Birth of Calvinist Millenarianism* (Dordrect, Netherlands: Kluwer, 2000).

13. Charles Daubuz, *A Perpetual Commentary on the Revelation of St. John* (London, 1720), and Moses Lowman, *A Paraphrase and Notes on the Revelation of St. John* (London, 1737).

14. Stephen J. Stein, "A Notebook on the Apocalypse by Jonathan Edwards," in *William and Mary Quarterly*, 3d ser., 29:4 (Oct. 1972). For a critical edition of Edwards's work on the second coming of Christ, see Jonathan Edwards, *Apocalyptic Writings*, ed. S. J. Stein (New Haven: Yale University Press, 1977).

15. David Lord, *The Coming of the Reign of Christ* (New York: 1858), 28ff.

16. Robert K. Whalen, "Millenarianism and Millennialism in America, 1790–1800" (unpublished Ph.D. Dissertation, State University of New York at Stony Brook, 1972), 17.

17. Hal Lindsey, *The Late Great Planet Earth* (Grand Rapids: Zondervan, 1970). Lindsey predicted the return of Christ in 1988, but, like all date setters, he had to so some quick revisions when Jesus did not appear as expected. The work of Leon Festinger and his cognitive dissonance theory is often used to explain the behavior of those who mistakenly set a date for the return of Christ. He claimed that when an individual held a cognition (belief or expec-

tation) that was later shown to be wrong, the person held the belief in a refocused form more strongly afterward. Festinger actually studied a religious group that predicted the world's end on a particular day and sold all their goods to prepare for the end. When the prediction failed, they believed even more strongly. See Leon Festinger, Henry W. Riecken, and Stanley Schacher, *When Prophecy Fails* (Minneapolis: University of Minnesota Press, 1956).

18. An interesting discussion of the complexities of dispensationalism may be found in Gleason Archer, *The Rapture: Pre-, Mid- or Post-Tribulational?* (Grand Rapids: Zondervan, 1984).

19. For a helpful study of the contrast between contemporary millennial systems, see Renald E. Showers, *There Really Is a Difference! A Comparison of Covenant and Dispensationalist Theology* (Bellmawr, NJ: The Friends of Israel Gospel Ministry, 1990).

20. C. S. Lewis, "The Christian Hope—Its Meaning for Today," in *Religion in Life* 21, no. 1 (Winter 1951–52): 30–31. The caution Lewis expresses with reference to the teaching of Christ's return should be taken seriously. Two books that give an objective analysis of extremist groups are Grace Halsell, *Prophecy and Politics, Militant Evangelicals on the Road to Nuclear War* (Westport, CT: Lawrence Hill and Co., 1986), and Anne Grace Mojtabi, *Blessed Assurance: At Home with the Bomb in Amarillo, Texas* (Boston: Houghton Mifflin, 1986).

Chapter 2—Premillennialism and the Church Fathers

"from the very beginning": The Church Fathers that we have discussed are those who are better known from a list of premillennialists that includes the following: from the Apostolic Fathers (those who were contemporary with or students of the apostles) Clement (fl. ca. 90–100), Papias (ca. 60–ca. 130/155), Polycarp (ca. 70–155/160), and Ignatius (d. ca. 98/117). Other works from this period include the *Didache*, *Epistle of Barnabas*, and *Shepherd of Hermas*. Those from the second century include: Justin Martyr (ca. 100–165), Irenaeus (ca. 120–ca. 202), the bishop of Lyons, and his disciple Hippolytus (d. ca. 236), Tertullian (150–225), Pothinus (ca. 87–177), Melito (d. ca. 190), Hegesippus (second century), Tatian (ca. 110–72), and Apollinaris (ca. 175). Those from the third century include: Cyprian (ca. 200–258), Commodianus (ca. 200–ca. 275), and Lactantius (ca. 240–ca. 320). Other less well known premillennialists are: Victorinus of Petau (d. ca. 304), Methodius (d. 311), Julius Africanus (d. ca. 240), Nepos (ca. 230–50), and Coracion (ca. 230–80). Two books that give a more complete view of early Christian eschatology are Brian E. Daily, *The Hope of the Early Church: A Handbook of Patristic Eschatology* (Peabody, MA: Hendrickson Publishers, 2003), and Charles E. Hill, *Regnum Caelorum: Patterns of Future Hope in Early Christianity* (Oxford: Oxford University Press, 1992).

FRAGMENTS OF PAPIAS

Papias, "Fragments of Papias," *The Writings of the Apostolic Fathers*, eds. A. Roberts, J. Donaldson and F. Crombie, (Edinburgh: T & T Clark, 1873), I, 443–45.

AGAINST THE HERETICS

Most of the millennial descriptions of Irenaeus are found in the closing chapters of his fifth book *Against the Heretics*. The translation of this book to which I referred was that found in vol. IX, 151ff. of the *Ante-Nicene Christian Library*, ed. A. Roberts and J. Donaldson (Edinburgh: T. & T. Clark, 1884) (hereafter cited as ANCL).

DIALOGUE WITH TRYPHO, A JEW

Justin Martyr, *Dialogue with Trypho, a Jew*, ANCL, II, 201–02.

THE FIVE BOOKS OF QUINTUS SEPT. FLOR.

Tertullian, *The Five Books of Quintus Sept. Flor. Against Marcion*, ANCL, VII, 170.

ON DANIEL

Hippolytus, *On Daniel*, ANCL, VI, 448.

THE INSTRUCTIONS OF COMMODIANUS IN FAVOUR OF CHRISTIAN DISCIPLINE, AGAINST THE GOD OF THE HEATHENS

Commodianus, *The Instructions of Commodianus in Favour of Christian Discipline, Against the God of the Heathens*, ANCL, XVIII, 456 F.

THE DIVINE INSTITUTES

Lactantius, *The Divine Institutes*, ANCL, XXI, 478–83.

DE PRINCIPIIS

Origen, *De Principiis*, ANCL, X, 145–47.

Chapter 3—Augustine's Spiritualized Amillennialism

THE CITY OF GOD

Augustine, *The City of God* in *A Select Library of the Nicene and Post-Nicene Fathers of the Christian Church*, ed. Philip Schaff (Grand Rapids: Eerdmans, 1949), II, 425–37.

Chapter 4—Radical Millenialist Movements and the Church's Response in the Medieval and Reformation Eras

ANABAPTIST MILLENNIALISM

Hans J. Hillerbrand, *The Reformation: A Narrative History Related by Contemporary Observers and Participants* (Grand Rapids: Baker, 1978), 253–63.

"the most fundamentally revolutionary element in the Christian tradition": Winston L. King, "Millennialism as a Social Ferment," in *Religion in Life* (Nashville: Abingdon Cokesbury Press, 1951–2), 33.

INSTITUTES OF THE CHRISTIAN RELIGION

John Calvin, *Institutes of the Christian Religion* (Edinburgh: The Calvin Translation Society, 1845), III, ed. Henry Beveridge, 25, 259–67.

John Calvin, *Joannis Calvini opera quae supersunt omnia*, ed. W. Baum, E. Cunitz, E. Reuss (Brunswigae: Schwetschke et Filium, 1889), XLI, 302–3.

  9. "malignant perverts": Heinrich Quistorp, *Calvin's Doctrine of the Last Things*, trans. Harold Knight (Richmond: John Knox Press, 1955), 158ff.

THE AUGSBURG CONFESSION

Philip Schaff, ed., *The Augsburg Confession, The Creeds of Christiandom with a History and Critical Notes* (New York: Harper, 1919), III, 16–18 (hereafter listed as Schaff).

THE BELGIC CONFESSION

Schaff, *The Belgic Confession*, III, 432–36.

THE SAVOY DECLARATION

Schaff, *The Savoy Declaration*, III, 720–23.

Chapter 5—Seventeenth-century Revival of Premillennialism

THE BELOVED CITY

Johann Heinrich Alsted, *The Beloved City* (London, 1643), 13.

THE KEY OF THE REVELATION

Joseph Mede, *The Key of the Revelation* (London, 1642).

THE PERSONALL REIGNE OF CHRIST UPON EARTH

John Archer, *The Personall Reigne of Christ upon Earth* (London, 1642), 103; 44–59.

FIFTH MONARCHY STATEMENTS

John Rogers, *Sarir: Or Doomes-day Drawing High with Thunder and Lightening to Lawyers* (1653). Excerpted in Edward Rogers, *Some Account of the Life and Opinions of a Fifth-Monarchy-Man* (London: Longmans, 1867), 82–98.

PROPHECIES

Anna Trapnel, *Prophecies*, in Champlin Burrage, "Anna Trapnel's Prophecies," *The English Historical Review* 26, 103 (July 1911): 526–35.

19. "an expression used elsewhere": Robert J. Leach, quoted in *Women in Ministry, Four Views*, ed. B. Clouse and R. G. Clouse (Downers Grove, IL: InterVarsity Press, 1987), 12.

Chapter 6—Eighteenth-century Postmillennialism

A PARAPHRASE AND COMMENTARY ON THE NEW TESTAMENT

Daniel Whitby, *A Paraphrase and Commentary on the New Testament* 10th ed., vol. 2 (London, 1807).

A HISTORY OF THE WORK OF REDEMPTION

Jonathan Edwards, *A History of the Work of Redemption* (London, 1774), 275–78, 328–33.

Chapter 7—Nineteenth-century Dispensationalism

LECTURES ON THE SECOND COMING

John Nelson Darby, *Lectures on the Second Coming* (London: G. Morrish, 1909), 1–7, 90–97.

THE BLACKSTONE MEMORIAL, 1891

William E. Blackstone, "The Blackstone Memorial, 1891," American Messianic Fellowship, www.amfi.org/blackmem.htm.

JESUS IS COMING

W. E. B. [William Eugene Blackstone], *Jesus Is Coming* (New York: Fleming H. Revell Co., 1932), 222–27, 228–32, 233–34, 234–36.

THE SECOND COMING OF CHRIST

Dwight L. Moody, *The Second Coming of Christ* (Chicago: Moody Press, 1896), 16–32.

Chapter 8—Twentieth-century Developments

ADDRESSES ON PROPHECY

C. I. [Cyrus Ingerson] Scofield, *Addresses on Prophecy* (Findlay, OH: Dunham Publishing Co., 1955), 107–123.

MUSSOLINI—POPE—"666"

William S. McBirnie, *Mussolini—Pope—"666"* (Veedersburg, IN: William S. McBirnie, n.d.), 23–35.

THE LORD COMETH, THE WORLD CRISIS EXPLAINED

Christabel Pankhurst, *The Lord Cometh: The World Crisis Explained* (London: Marshall, Morgan and Scott, 1934), VIII–XI, 23–30.

SEEING THE FUTURE

Christabel Pankhurst, *Seeing the Future* (New York: Harper & Brothers Publishers, 1929).

THE RESURRECTION OF THE OLD ROMAN EMPIRE, THE LEAGUE OF NATIONS AND THE FUTURE OF EUROPE

Leonard Sale-Harrison, *The Resurrection of the Old Roman Empire, The League of Nations and the Future of Europe* (London: Pickering and Inglis, 1940), 106–121.

THE "MOUNTAIN PEAKS" OF PROPHECY

Clarence Larkin, *The Second Coming of Christ* (Glenside, PA: Rev. Clarence Larkin Estate, 1922), 3, 5, 36–37, 46, 50.

Chapter 9—Into the Twenty-first Century

THE LATE GREAT PLANET EARTH

Hal Lindsey, *The Late Great Planet Earth* (Grand Rapids: Zondervan, 1970, 1977; New York: Inspirational Press, 1994), 6, 12, 20, 50, 67–69, 83–86, 90, 104, 135. Citations are to the Inspirational Press reprinted edition.

"scattered in bits throughout the Old and New Testaments": *The Late Great Planet Earth* (Grand Rapids: Zondervan, 1970, 1977; New York: Inspirational Press, 1994), 31. Citation is to the Inspirational Press reprinted edition.

"this tendency is even more evident": *Apocalypse Code* (Palos Verdes, CA: Western Front, 1997), 36–37ff.

LEFT BEHIND

Tim LaHaye and Jerry B. Jenkins, *Left Behind* (Wheaton, IL: Tyndale, 1995), 16, 62, 79–80, 99, 118–19, 121, 123, 166, 195–203, 214, 310.

Glossary ☐

The defintions in this glossary are broadly acceptable in the dispensation-alist tradition, though particular interpretations may vary.

144,000: A group of 12,000 Jews descended from each of the twelve tribes of Israel who will become evangelists, winning many of those who are "left behind" during the tribulation to faith in Christ (Rev. 7:4).

Abrahamic covenant: An agreement between Abraham and God promising the patriarch land, descendants, and unconditional blessings (Gen. 15, 17).

amillennialism: The view held by most of the major denominations that there will not be a future millennial reign of Christ on earth.

Antichrist: Refers to the spirit of evil in opposition to Christ and to a world ruler who will come on the scene at the end of the age. Revelation 12–13 presents an unholy trinity that aligns Satan, the Antichrist and the false prophet.

apocalypticism: A type of highly symbolic literature that reveals coming events, found in the Hebrew Bible and New Testament as well as in extracanonical Jewish and Christian writings from the period 200 B.C.E.–200 C.E.

Babylon: Ancient city located fifty miles south of modern Baghdad. Some scholars believe it is a term used to represent the epitome of corrupt human society and thus, in the book of Revelation, could refer to Rome. Others feel that Babylon will be rebuilt during the tribulation period and that the Antichrist will rule the world from there.

chiliasm: see ***premillennialism***.

church age: The period beginning on the day of Pentecost (Acts 2) and ending with the rapture of the church before the tribulation period.

Davidic covenant: Enlarges on the Abrahamic covenant and promises that the kingdom of Israel will be eternal (2 Sam. 7, Ps. 89).

dispensationalism: A system of theology which teaches that God relates to humanity through a series of distinct epochs. Often there are believed to be seven of these dispensations, as taught in the *Scofield Reference Bible*.

eschatology: The study of the last things, of end-times events. It includes the consummation of the kingdom of God with events such as the rapture, the millennium, the conversion of Israel, the last judgment and the eternal state.

Gog and Magog: Ezekiel 38–39 describes a great invasion of Israel in the latter days by a great confederation of nations. Gog is often identified as the leader of this confederation and Magog is the Central Asian component, which includes the Islamic republics of the former Soviet empire.

imminent: This term is applied to the rapture of the church, meaning that Christ could return at any moment. No biblically predicted even must precede his coming.

judgment of the nations: Dispensationalists believe in a series of eschatological judgments. This particular one will occur immediately prior to the start of the millennial kingdom. These nations (or Gentiles) are judged according to the terms described in Matthew 25—that is, their treatment of the Jews during the tribulation period.

judgment seat of Christ: The judgment at which believers in Christ will receive rewards in proportion to their service to God (Luke 19:11–27).

last days: A reference to the current church dispensation or to the future culmination of God's plan for Israel.

mark of the beast: During the tribulation period every person will be required to receive a visible mark of "666," which signifies loyalty to the Antichrist and enables the beast to control all commerce and worship (Rev. 13:16–18, 14:9–11, 16:2, 19:20, 20:4).

postmillennialism: The belief that the return of Christ will take place after the millennium, which may be a literal period of peace and prosperity or else a symbolic representation of the final triumph of the gospel. The new age will come through Christian teaching and preaching and will not necessarily last 1,000 years because the number can be interpreted symbolically.

premillennialism: Also called "chiliasm," it is the belief that there will be a literal 1,000-year reign of Christ on earth at the end of the present age. This millennium will be a time of unparalleled justice, peace, prosperity, and righteousness. This teaching is based on Revelation 20:1–10 and is expanded upon using Hebrew Bible passages such as Isaiah 55–66.

pretribulationism: The premillenialist view that the rapture, the event in which the church will be literally "caught up" in the air to meet Christ, will occur at the beginning of the tribulation period (1 Thess. 4:15–17). Historically, premillennialists have divided over whether the rapter will occur before (pretribulationism), during (midtribulationism), or after (posttribulationism) the seven-year time of trouble upon the earth (Dan. 9:24-27).

progressive dispensationalism: a recent development whose adherents wish to change dispensationalism by emphasizing the importance of the church rather than Israel in God's plan, and by less concentration on the details of the second coming of Christ.

typology: A method of interpretation whereby various persons, events, or institutions in the Hebrew Bible are seen as foreshadowing a greater spiritual reality in the New Testament, often corresponding to some aspect of Christ or his ministry. Hence, Adam is a type of Christ, the "last Adam" (1 Cor. 15:45–49) and Passover is a type of Christ's own sacrifice as the new Passover lamb (1 Cor. 5:7). Jesus emphasized that the entire Hebrew Bible was given to reflect and portary his many-faceted ministry (Luke 24:25–44, John 5:39-44).

Suggestions for Further Reading □

Armerding, Carl E., and W. Ward Gasque, eds. *Handbook of Biblical Prophecy.* Grand Rapids: Baker, 1977.

Barkun, Michael. *Disaster and the Millennium.* New Haven: Yale University Press, 1974.

Bass, Clarence B. *Backgrounds to Dispensationalism.* Grand Rapids: Baker, 1960.

Boyer, Paul. *When Time Shall Be No More: Prophecy Belief in Modern American Culture.* Cambridge: Harvard University Press, 1992.

Brown, Peter. *Augustine of Hippo: A Biography.* Berkeley: University of California Press, 1969.

Capp, B. S. *The Fifth Monarchy Men: A Study in Seventeenth-Century English Millenarianism.* Totowa, NJ: Rowman and Littlefield, 1972.

Carpenter, Joel A. *Revive Us Again: The Reawakening of American Fundamentalism.* New York: Oxford University Press, 1997.

Chadwick, Henry. *Augustine.* Oxford: Oxford University Press, 1986.

Clouse, Robert G., ed. *The Meaning of the Millennium.* Downers Grove, IL: InterVarsity Press, 1977.

Couch, Mal, ed. *Dictionary of Premillennial Theology.* Grand Rapids: Kregel, 1996.

Daily, Brian E. *The Hope of the Early Church: A Handbook of Patristic Eschatology.* Peabody, MA: Hendrickson Publishers, 2003.

Davidson, James West. *The Logic of Millennial Thought.* New Haven: Yale University Press, 1977.

DeJong, James A. *As the Waters Cover the Sea: Millennial Expectations in the Rise of Anglo-American Missions 1640–1810.* Kampen, Netherlands: J. H. Kok, 1970.

Erickson, Millard J. *Contemporary Options in Eschatology: A Study of the Millennium.* Grand Rapids: Baker, 1977.

Festinger, Leon, Henry W. Riecken, and Stanley Schacher. *When Prophecy Fails.* Minneapolis: University of Minnesota Press, 1956.

Firth, Katherine R. *The Apocalyptic Tradition in Reformation Britain, 1530–1645.* Oxford: Oxford University Press, 1979.

Froom, LeRoy Edwin. *The Prophetic Faith of Our Fathers.* 4 vols. Washington: Review and Herald, 1954.

Fuller, Robert. *Naming the Antichrist: The History of an American Obsession*. New York: Oxford University Press, 1995.

Garrett, Clarke. *Respectable Folly: Millenarians and the French Revolution in France and England*. Baltimore: Johns Hopkins University Press, 1975.

Grenz, Stanley J. *The Millennial Maze: Sorting Out Evangelical Options*. Downers Grove, IL: InterVarsity Press, 1992.

Hill, Charles E. *Regnum Caelorum: Patterns of Future Hope in Early Christianity*. Oxford: Oxford University Press, 1992.

Hillerbrand, Hans J. *The Reformation: A Narrative History Related by Contemporary Observers and Participants*. Grand Rapids: Baker, 1978.

Hoekema, Anthony A. *The Bible and the Future*. Grand Rapids: Eerdmans, 1979.

Kromminga, D. H. *The Millennium in the Church*. Grand Rapids: Eerdmans, 1945.

LaHaye, Tim F. and Jerry B. Jenkins. *Left Behind: A Novel of the Earth's Last Days*. Wheaton: Tyndale House Publishing, 1995.

Larkin, Clarence. *Dispensational Truth or God's Plan and Purpose in the Ages*. Santa Fe, NM: Sun Publishing, 1998.

Lindsey, Hal. *The Late Great Planet Earth*. Grand Rapids: Zondervan, 1970.

———. *Satan Is Alive and Well on Planet Earth*. Grand Rapids: Zondervan, 1972.

Marsden, George. *Fundamentalism and American Culture*. New York: Oxford University Press, 1980.

McGinn, Bernard. *Visions of the End*. New York: Columbia University Press, 1979.

Numbers, Ronald L., and Jonathan M. Butler. *The Disappointed*. Knoxville: University of Tennessee Press, 1993.

O'Leary, Stephen D. *Arguing the Apocalypse: A Theory of Millennial Rhetoric*. New York: Oxford University Press, 1994.

Peters, George N. H. *The Theocratic Kingdom of Our Lord Jesus Christ*. 3 vols. Grand Rapids: Kregel, 1979.

Ryrie, Charles C. *The Bible and Tomorrow's News*. Wheaton, IL: Scripture Press, 1969.

———. *Dispensationalism*. Chicago: Moody Press, 1995.

Sandeen, Ernest R. *The Roots of Fundamentalism*. Chicago: University of Chicago Press, 1970.

Schmithals, Walter. *The Apocalyptic Movement*. Nashville: Abingdon Press, 1975.

Scott, Kermit T. *Augustine: His Thought in Context*. Mahwah, NJ: Paulist, 1995.

Stone, Jon R. *A Guide to the End of the World: Popular Eschatology In America*. New York: Garland, 1993.

Travis, Stephen. *I Believe in the Second Coming of Jesus*. Grand Rapids: Eerdmans, 1982.

Tuveson, Ernest Lee. *Millennium and Utopia*. New York: Harper, 1964.

————. *Redeemer Nation: The Idea of America's Millennial Role*. Chicago: University of Chicago Press, 1968.

Van der Meer, F. *Augustine the Bishop: The Life and Work of a Father of the Church*. Translated by Brian Battershaw and G. R. Lamb. London: Sheed and Ward, 1961.

Wainwright, Arthur W. *Mysterious Apocalypse: Interpreting the Book of Revelation*. Nashville: Abingdon Press, 1993.

Weber, Timothy P. *Living in the Shadow of the Second Coming*. Chicago: University of Chicago Press, 1987.

————. *On the Road to Armageddon: How Evangelicals Became Israel's Best Friend*. Grand Rapids: Baker Academic, 2004.

Wilcock, Michael. *I Saw Heaven Opened: The Message of Revelation*. Downers Grove, IL: InterVarsity Press, 1975.

Williams, Michael D. *This World Is Not My Home: The Origins and Development of Dispensationalism*. Fearn, Ross-Shire, Scotland: Christian Focus Publications, 2003.

Wilson, Dwight. *Armageddon Now! The Premillenarian Response to Russia and Israel since 1917*. Grand Rapids: Baker, 1977.

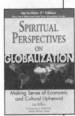

Midrash Fiction / Folktales

Abraham's Bind & Other Bible Tales of Trickery, Folly, Mercy and Love by Michael J. Caduto

New retellings of episodes in the lives of familiar biblical characters explore relevant life lessons.

6 x 9, 224 pp, HC, 978-1-59473-186-0 **$19.99**

Daughters of the Desert: Stories of Remarkable Women from Christian, Jewish and Muslim Traditions by Claire Rudolf Murphy, Meghan Nuttall Sayres, Mary Cronk Farrell, Sarah Conover and Betsy Wharton

Breathes new life into the old tales of our female ancestors in faith. Uses traditional scriptural passages as starting points, then with vivid detail fills in historical context and place. Chapters reveal the voices of Sarah, Hagar, Huldah, Esther, Salome, Mary Magdalene, Lydia, Khadija, Fatima and many more. Historical fiction ideal for readers of all ages. Quality paperback includes reader's discussion guide.

5½ x 8½, 192 pp, Quality PB, 978-1-59473-106-8 **$14.99**
HC, 192 pp, 978-1-893361-72-0 **$19.95**

The Triumph of Eve & Other Subversive Bible Tales
by Matt Biers-Ariel

Many people were taught and remember only a one-dimensional Bible. These engaging retellings are the antidote to this—they're witty, often hilarious, always profound, and invite you to grapple with questions and issues that are often hidden in the original text.

5½ x 8½, 192 pp, Quality PB, 978-1-59473-176-1 **$14.99**
HC, 192 pp, 978-1-59473-040-5 **$19.99**

Also avail.: **The Triumph of Eve Teacher's Guide**
8½ x 11, 44 pp, PB, 978-1-59473-152-5 **$8.99**

Wisdom in the Telling
Finding Inspiration and Grace in Traditional Folktales and Myths Retold
by Lorraine Hartin-Gelardi
6 x 9, 224 pp, HC, 978-1-59473-185-3 **$19.99**

Religious Etiquette / Reference

How to Be a Perfect Stranger, 4th Edition: The Essential Religious Etiquette Handbook Edited by Stuart M. Matlins and Arthur J. Magida

The indispensable guidebook to help the well-meaning guest when visiting other people's religious ceremonies. A straightforward guide to the rituals and celebrations of the major religions and denominations in the United States and Canada from the perspective of an interested guest of any other faith, based on information obtained from authorities of each religion. Belongs in every living room, library and office. Covers:

African American Methodist Churches • Assemblies of God • Bahá'í • Baptist • Buddhist • Christian Church (Disciples of Christ) • Christian Science (Church of Christ, Scientist) • Churches of Christ • Episcopalian and Anglican • Hindu • Islam • Jehovah's Witnesses • Jewish • Lutheran • Mennonite/Amish • Methodist • Mormon (Church of Jesus Christ of Latter-day Saints) • Native American/First Nations • Orthodox Churches • Pentecostal Church of God • Presbyterian • Quaker (Religious Society of Friends) • Reformed Church in America/Canada • Roman Catholic • Seventh-day Adventist • Sikh • Unitarian Universalist • United Church of Canada • United Church of Christ

6 x 9, 432 pp, Quality PB, 978-1-59473-140-2 **$19.99**

The Perfect Stranger's Guide to Funerals and Grieving Practices: A Guide to Etiquette in Other People's Religious Ceremonies Edited by Stuart M. Matlins
6 x 9, 240 pp, Quality PB, 978-1-893361-20-1 **$16.95**

The Perfect Stranger's Guide to Wedding Ceremonies: A Guide to Etiquette in Other People's Religious Ceremonies Edited by Stuart M. Matlins
6 x 9, 208 pp, Quality PB, 978-1-893361-19-5 **$16.95**

Kabbalah from Jewish Lights Publishing

Awakening to Kabbalah: The Guiding Light of Spiritual Fulfillment
by Rav Michael Laitman, PhD 6 x 9, 192 pp, HC, 978-1-58023-264-7 **$21.99**

Cast in God's Image: Discover Your Personality Type Using the Enneagram and Kabbalah
by Rabbi Howard A. Addison 7 x 9, 176 pp, Quality PB, 978-1-58023-124-4 **$16.95**

Ehyeh: A Kabbalah for Tomorrow *by Dr. Arthur Green*
6 x 9, 224 pp, Quality PB, 978-1-58023-213-5 **$16.99**

The Enneagram and Kabbalah, 2nd Edition: Reading Your Soul
by Rabbi Howard A. Addison 6 x 9, 192 pp, Quality PB, 978-1-58023-229-6 **$16.99**

Finding Joy: A Practical Spiritual Guide to Happiness *by Dannel I. Schwartz with Mark Hass*
6 x 9, 192 pp, Quality PB, 978-1-58023-009-4 **$14.95**

The Gift of Kabbalah: Discovering the Secrets of Heaven, Renewing Your Life on Earth
by Tamar Frankiel, PhD 6 x 9, 256 pp, Quality PB, 978-1-58023-141-1 **$16.95**
HC, 978-1-58023-108-4 **$21.95**

Honey from the Rock: An Easy Introduction to Jewish Mysticism
by Lawrence Kushner 6 x 9, 176 pp, Quality PB, 978-1-58023-073-5 **$16.95**

Kabbalah: A Brief Introduction for Christians
by Tamar Frankiel, PhD 5½ x 8½, 176 pp, Quality PB, 978-1-58023-303-3 **$16.99**

Zohar: Annotated & Explained *Translation and Annotation by Dr. Daniel C. Matt*
Foreword by Andrew Harvey 5½ x 8½, 176 pp, Quality PB, 978-1-893361-51-5 **$15.99**

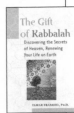

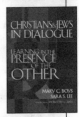

Judaism / Christianity

Christians and Jews in Dialogue: Learning in the Presence of the Other
by Mary C. Boys and Sara S. Lee; Foreword by Dorothy C. Bass
Inspires renewed commitment to dialogue between religious traditions and illuminates how it should happen. Explains the transformative work of creating environments for Jews and Christians to study together and enter the dynamism of the other's religious tradition.
6 x 9, 240 pp, HC, 978-1-59473-144-0 **$21.99**

Healing the Jewish-Christian Rift: Growing Beyond Our Wounded History
by Ron Miller and Laura Bernstein; Foreword by Dr. Beatrice Bruteau
6 x 9, 288 pp, Quality PB, 978-1-59473-139-6 **$18.99**

Introducing My Faith and My Community
The Jewish Outreach Institute Guide for the Christian in a Jewish Interfaith Relationship
by Rabbi Kerry M. Olitzky 6 x 9, 176 pp, Quality PB, 978-1-58023-192-3 **$16.99** *(a Jewish Lights book)*

The Jewish Approach to God: A Brief Introduction for Christians
by Rabbi Neil Gillman 5½ x 8½, 192 pp, Quality PB, 978-1-58023-190-9 **$16.95** *(a Jewish Lights book)*

Jewish Holidays: A Brief Introduction for Christians
by Rabbi Kerry M. Olitzky and Rabbi Daniel Judson
5½ x 8½, 176 pp, Quality PB, 978-1-58023-302-6 **$16.99** *(a Jewish Lights book)*

Jewish Ritual: A Brief Introduction for Christians
by Rabbi Kerry M. Olitzky and Rabbi Daniel Judson
5½ x 8½, 144 pp, Quality PB, 978-1-58023-210-4 **$14.99** *(a Jewish Lights book)*

Jewish Spirituality: A Brief Introduction for Christians
by Rabbi Lawrence Kushner
5½ x 8½, 112 pp, Quality PB, 978-1-58023-150-3 **$12.95** *(a Jewish Lights book)*

A Jewish Understanding of the New Testament
by Rabbi Samuel Sandmel; new Preface by Rabbi David Sandmel
5½ x 8½, 368 pp, Quality PB, 978-1-59473-048-1 **$19.99**

We Jews and Jesus
Exploring Theological Differences for Mutual Understanding
by Rabbi Samuel Sandmel; new Preface by Rabbi David Sandmel A Classic Reprint
Written in a non-technical way for the layperson, this candid and forthright look at the what and why of the Jewish attitude toward Jesus is a clear and forceful exposition that guides both Christians and Jews in relevant discussion.
6 x 9, 192 pp, Quality PB, 978-1-59473-208-9 **$16.99**

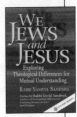

Spiritual Biography—SkyLight Lives

SkyLight Lives reintroduces the lives and works of key spiritual figures of our time—people who by their teaching or example have challenged our assumptions about spirituality and have caused us to look at it in new ways.

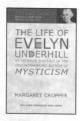 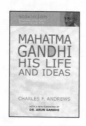  

The Life of Evelyn Underhill
An Intimate Portrait of the Groundbreaking Author of *Mysticism*
by Margaret Cropper; Foreword by Dana Greene
Evelyn Underhill was a passionate writer and teacher who wrote elegantly on mysticism, worship, and devotional life.
6 x 9, 288 pp, 5 b/w photos, Quality PB, 978-1-893361-70-6 **$18.95**

Mahatma Gandhi: His Life and Ideas
by Charles F. Andrews; Foreword by Dr. Arun Gandhi
Examines from a contemporary Christian activist's point of view the religious ideas and political dynamics that influenced the birth of the peaceful resistance movement.
6 x 9, 336 pp, 5 b/w photos, Quality PB, 978-1-893361-89-8 **$18.95**

Simone Weil: A Modern Pilgrimage
by Robert Coles
The extraordinary life of the spiritual philosopher who's been called both saint and madwoman.
6 x 9, 208 pp, Quality PB, 978-1-893361-34-8 **$16.95**

Zen Effects: The Life of Alan Watts
by Monica Furlong
Through his widely popular books and lectures, Alan Watts (1915–1973) did more to introduce Eastern philosophy and religion to Western minds than any figure before or since.
6 x 9, 264 pp, Quality PB, 978-1-893361-32-4 **$16.95**

More Spiritual Biography

Bede Griffiths: An Introduction to His Interspiritual Thought
by Wayne Teasdale
The first study of his contemplative experience and thought, exploring the intersection of Hinduism and Christianity.
6 x 9, 288 pp, Quality PB, 978-1-893361-77-5 **$18.95**

The Soul of the Story: Meetings with Remarkable People
by Rabbi David Zeller
Inspiring and entertaining, this compelling collection of spiritual adventures assures us that no spiritual lesson truly learned is ever lost.
6 x 9, 288 pp, HC, 978-1-58023-272-2 **$21.99** *(a Jewish Lights book)*

Meditation / Prayer

Prayers to an Evolutionary God
by William Cleary; Afterword by Diarmuid O'Murchu

How is it possible to pray when God is dislocated from heaven, dispersed all around us, and more of a creative force than an all-knowing father? Inspired by the spiritual and scientific teachings of Diarmuid O'Murchu and Teilhard de Chardin, Cleary reveals that religion and science can be combined to create an expanding view of the universe—an evolutionary faith.
6 x 9, 208 pp, HC, 978-1-59473-006-1 **$21.99**

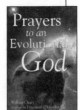

Psalms: A Spiritual Commentary
by M. Basil Pennington, ocso; Illustrations by Phillip Ratner

Showing how the Psalms give profound and candid expression to both our highest aspirations and our deepest pain, the late, highly respected Cistercian Abbot M. Basil Pennington shares his reflections on some of the most beloved passages from the Bible's most widely read book.
6 x 9, 176 pp, HC, 24 full-page b/w illus., 978-1-59473-141-9 **$19.99**

The Song of Songs: A Spiritual Commentary
by M. Basil Pennington, ocso; Illustrations by Phillip Ratner

Join the late M. Basil Pennington as he ruminates on the Bible's most challenging mystical text. Follow a path into the Songs that weaves through his inspired words and the evocative drawings of Jewish artist Phillip Ratner—a path that reveals your own humanity and leads to the deepest delight of your soul.
6 x 9, 160 pp, HC, 14 b/w illus., 978-1-59473-004-7 **$19.99**

Women of Color Pray: Voices of Strength, Faith, Healing, Hope and Courage
Edited and with Introductions by Christal M. Jackson

Through these prayers, poetry, lyrics, meditations and affirmations, you will share in the strong and undeniable connection women of color share with God. It will challenge you to explore new ways of prayerful expression.
5 x 7¼, 208 pp, Quality PB, 978-1-59473-077-1 **$15.99**

The Art of Public Prayer: Not for Clergy Only
by Lawrence A. Hoffman

An ecumenical resource for all people looking to change hardened worship patterns.
6 x 9, 288 pp, Quality PB, 978-1-893361-06-5 **$18.99**

Finding Grace at the Center: The Beginning of Centering Prayer
by M. Basil Pennington, ocso, Thomas Keating, ocso, and Thomas E. Clarke, sj
5 x 7¼, 112 pp, HC, 978-1-893361-69-0 **$14.95**

A Heart of Stillness: A Complete Guide to Learning the Art of Meditation
by David A. Cooper 5½ x 8½, 272 pp, Quality PB, 978-1-893361-03-4 **$16.95**

Meditation without Gurus: A Guide to the Heart of Practice
by Clark Strand 5½ x 8½, 192 pp, Quality PB, 978-1-893361-93-5 **$16.95**

Praying with Our Hands: 21 Practices of Embodied Prayer from the World's
Spiritual Traditions *by Jon M. Sweeney; Photographs by Jennifer J. Wilson; Foreword by Mother Tessa Bielecki; Afterword by Taitetsu Unno, PhD*
8 x 8, 96 pp, 22 duotone photos, Quality PB, 978-1-893361-16-4 **$16.95**

Silence, Simplicity & Solitude: A Complete Guide to Spiritual Retreat at Home
by David A. Cooper 5½ x 8½, 336 pp, Quality PB, 978-1-893361-04-1 **$16.95**

Three Gates to Meditation Practice: A Personal Journey into Sufism, Buddhism, and Judaism
by David A. Cooper 5½ x 8½, 240 pp, Quality PB, 978-1-893361-22-5 **$16.95**

Women Pray: Voices through the Ages, from Many Faiths, Cultures and Traditions
Edited and with Introductions by Monica Furlong
5 x 7¼, 256 pp, Quality PB, 978-1-59473-071-9 **$15.99**
Deluxe HC with ribbon marker, 978-1-893361-25-6 **$19.95**

Spirituality

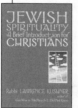

Jewish Spirituality: A Brief Introduction for Christians   *by Lawrence Kushner*
5½ x 8½, 112 pp, Quality PB, 978-1-58023-150-3 **$12.95** *(a Jewish Lights book)*

Journeys of Simplicity: Traveling Light with Thomas Merton, Bashō, Edward Abbey, Annie Dillard & Others   *by Philip Harnden* 5 x 7¼, 128 pp, HC, 978-1-893361-76-8 **$16.95**

Keeping Spiritual Balance As We Grow Older: More than 65 Creative Ways to Use Purpose, Prayer, and the Power of Spirit to Build a Meaningful Retirement
by Molly and Bernie Srode 8 x 8, 224 pp, Quality PB, 978-1-59473-042-9 **$16.99**

The Monks of Mount Athos: A Western Monk's Extraordinary Spiritual Journey on Eastern Holy Ground   *by M. Basil Pennington, ocso; Foreword by Archimandrite Dionysios*
6 x 9, 256 pp, 10+ b/w line drawings, Quality PB, 978-1-893361-78-2 **$18.95**

One God Clapping: The Spiritual Path of a Zen Rabbi   *by Alan Lew with Sherrill Jaffe*
5½ x 8½, 336 pp, Quality PB, 978-1-58023-115-2 **$16.95** *(a Jewish Lights book)*

Prayer for People Who Think Too Much: A Guide to Everyday, Anywhere Prayer from the World's Faith Traditions   *by Mitch Finley*
5½ x 8½, 224 pp, Quality PB, 978-1-893361-21-8 **$16.99**; HC, 978-1-893361-00-3 **$21.95**

Show Me Your Way: The Complete Guide to Exploring Interfaith Spiritual Direction
by Howard A. Addison   5½ x 8½, 240 pp, Quality PB, 978-1-893361-41-6 **$16.95**

Spirituality 101: The Indispensable Guide to Keeping—or Finding—Your Spiritual Life on Campus   *by Harriet L. Schwartz, with contributions from college students at nearly thirty campuses across the United States* 6 x 9, 272 pp, Quality PB, 978-1-59473-000-9 **$16.99**

Spiritually Incorrect: Finding God in All the Wrong Places   *by Dan Wakefield; Illus. by Marian DelVecchio* 5½ x 8½, 192 pp, b/w illus., Quality PB, 978-1-59473-137-2 **$15.99**

Spiritual Manifestos: Visions for Renewed Religious Life in America from Young Spiritual Leaders of Many Faiths   *Edited by Niles Elliot Goldstein; Preface by Martin E. Marty*
6 x 9, 256 pp, HC, 978-1-893361-09-6 **$21.95**

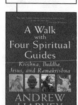

A Walk with Four Spiritual Guides: Krishna, Buddha, Jesus, and Ramakrishna
by Andrew Harvey 5½ x 8½, 192 pp, 10 b/w photos & illus., Quality PB, 978-1-59473-138-9 **$15.99**

What Matters: Spiritual Nourishment for Head and Heart
by Frederick Franck 5 x 7¼, 128 pp, 50+ b/w illus., HC, 978-1-59473-013-9 **$16.99**

Who Is My God?, 2nd Edition: An Innovative Guide to Finding Your Spiritual Identity
Created by the Editors at SkyLight Paths 6 x 9, 160 pp, Quality PB, 978-1-59473-014-6 **$15.99**

Spirituality—A Week Inside

Come and Sit: A Week Inside Meditation Centers
by Marcia Z. Nelson; Foreword by Wayne Teasdale
The insider's guide to meditation in a variety of different spiritual traditions—Buddhist, Hindu, Christian, Jewish, and Sufi traditions.
6 x 9, 224 pp, b/w photos, Quality PB, 978-1-893361-35-5 **$16.95**

Lighting the Lamp of Wisdom: A Week Inside a Yoga Ashram
by John Ittner; Foreword by Dr. David Frawley
This insider's guide to Hindu spiritual life takes you into a typical week of retreat inside a yoga ashram to demystify the experience and show you what to expect.
6 x 9, 192 pp, 10+ b/w photos, Quality PB, 978-1-893361-52-2 **$15.95**

Making a Heart for God: A Week Inside a Catholic Monastery
by Dianne Aprile; Foreword by Brother Patrick Hart, ocso
Takes you to the Abbey of Gethsemani—the Trappist monastery in Kentucky that was home to author Thomas Merton—to explore the details.
6 x 9, 224 pp, b/w photos, Quality PB, 978-1-893361-49-2 **$16.95**

Waking Up: A Week Inside a Zen Monastery
by Jack Maguire; Foreword by John Daido Loori, Roshi
An essential guide to what it's like to spend a week inside a Zen Buddhist monastery.
6 x 9, 224 pp, b/w photos, Quality PB, 978-1-893361-55-3 **$16.95**
HC, 978-1-893361-13-3 **$21.95**

Spiritual Poetry—The Mystic Poets

Experience these mystic poets as you never have before. Each beautiful, compact book includes: a brief introduction to the poet's time and place; a summary of the major themes of the poet's mysticism and religious tradition; essential selections from the poet's most important works; and an appreciative preface by a contemporary spiritual writer.

 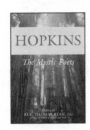  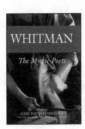

Hafiz: The Mystic Poets
Preface by Ibrahim Gamard
Hafiz is known throughout the world as Persia's greatest poet, with sales of his poems in Iran today only surpassed by those of the Qur'an itself. His probing and joyful verse speaks to people from all backgrounds who long to taste and feel divine love and experience harmony with all living things.
5 x 7¼, 144 pp, HC, 978-1-59473-009-2 **$16.99**

Hopkins: The Mystic Poets
Preface by Rev. Thomas Ryan, CSP
Gerard Manley Hopkins, Christian mystical poet, is beloved for his use of fresh language and startling metaphors to describe the world around him. Although his verse is lovely, beneath the surface lies a searching soul, wrestling with and yearning for God.
5 x 7¼, 112 pp, HC, 978-1-59473-010-8 **$16.99**

Tagore: The Mystic Poets
Preface by Swami Adiswarananda
Rabindranath Tagore is often considered the "Shakespeare" of modern India. A great mystic, Tagore was the teacher of W. B. Yeats and Robert Frost, the close friend of Albert Einstein and Mahatma Gandhi, and the winner of the Nobel Prize for Literature. This beautiful sampling of Tagore's two most important works, *The Gardener* and *Gitanjali,* offers a glimpse into his spiritual vision that has inspired people around the world.
5 x 7¼, 144 pp, HC, 978-1-59473-008-5 **$16.99**

Whitman: The Mystic Poets
Preface by Gary David Comstock
Walt Whitman was the most innovative and influential poet of the nineteenth century. This beautiful sampling of Whitman's most important poetry from *Leaves of Grass,* and selections from his prose writings, offers a glimpse into the spiritual side of his most radical themes—love for country, love for others, and love of Self.
5 x 7¼, 192 pp, HC, 978-1-59473-041-2 **$16.99**

Spirituality & Crafts

The Knitting Way: A Guide to Spiritual Self-Discovery
by Linda Skolnik and Janice MacDaniels
7 x 9, 240 pp, Quality PB, 978-1-59473-079-5 **$16.99**

The Quilting Path
A Guide to Spiritual Discovery through Fabric, Thread and Kabbalah
by Louise Silk
7 x 9, 192 pp, Quality PB, 978-1-59473-206-5 **$16.99**

Spiritual Practice

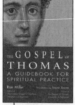

Divining the Body
Reclaim the Holiness of Your Physical Self *by Jan Phillips*
A practical and inspiring guidebook for connecting the body and soul in spiritual practice. Leads you into a milieu of reverence, mystery and delight, helping you discover your body as a pathway to the Divine.
8 x 8, 256 pp, Quality PB, 978-1-59473-080-1 **$16.99**

Finding Time for the Timeless: Spirituality in the Workweek
by John McQuiston II
Simple, refreshing stories that provide you with examples of how you can refocus and enrich your daily life using prayer or meditation, ritual and other forms of spiritual practice. 5½ x 6¼, 208 pp, HC, 978-1-59473-035-1 **$17.99**

The Gospel of Thomas
A Guidebook for Spiritual Practice *by Ron Miller; Translations by Stevan Davies*
An innovative guide to bring a new spiritual classic into daily life.
6 x 9, 160 pp, Quality PB, 978-1-59473-047-4 **$14.99**

Earth, Water, Fire, and Air: Essential Ways of Connecting to Spirit
by Cait Johnson 6 x 9, 224 pp, HC, 978-1-893361-65-2 **$19.95**

Labyrinths from the Outside In: Walking to Spiritual Insight—A Beginner's Guide
by Donna Schaper and Carole Ann Camp
6 x 9, 208 pp, b/w illus. and photos, Quality PB, 978-1-893361-18-8 **$16.95**

Practicing the Sacred Art of Listening: A Guide to Enrich Your Relationships and Kindle Your Spiritual Life—The Listening Center Workshop
by Kay Lindahl 8 x 8, 176 pp, Quality PB, 978-1-893361-85-0 **$16.95**

Releasing the Creative Spirit: Unleash the Creativity in Your Life
by Dan Wakefield 7 x 10, 256 pp, Quality PB, 978-1-893361-36-2 **$16.95**

The Sacred Art of Bowing: Preparing to Practice
by Andi Young 5½ x 8½, 128 pp, b/w illus., Quality PB, 978-1-893361-82-9 **$14.95**

The Sacred Art of Chant: Preparing to Practice
by Ana Hernández 5½ x 8½, 192 pp, Quality PB, 978-1-59473-036-8 **$15.99**

The Sacred Art of Fasting: Preparing to Practice
by Thomas Ryan, CSP 5½ x 8½, 192 pp, Quality PB, 978-1-59473-078-8 **$15.99**

The Sacred Art of Forgiveness: Forgiving Ourselves and Others through God's Grace
by Marcia Ford 8 x 8, 176 pp, Quality PB, 978-1-59473-175-4 **$16.99**

The Sacred Art of Listening: Forty Reflections for Cultivating a Spiritual Practice
by Kay Lindahl; Illustrations by Amy Schnapper
8 x 8, 160 pp, b/w illus., Quality PB, 978-1-893361-44-7 **$16.99**

The Sacred Art of Lovingkindness: Preparing to Practice
by Rabbi Rami Shapiro; Foreword by Marcia Ford
5½ x 8½, 176 pp, Quality PB, 978-1-59473-151-8 **$16.99**

Sacred Speech: A Practical Guide for Keeping Spirit in Your Speech
by Rev. Donna Schaper 6 x 9, 176 pp, Quality PB, 978-1-59473-068-9 **$15.99**
HC, 978-1-893361-74-4 **$21.95**

Spirituality of the Seasons

Autumn: A Spiritual Biography of the Season
Edited by Gary Schmidt and Susan M. Felch; Illustrations by Mary Azarian
Rejoice in autumn as a time of preparation and reflection. Includes Wendell Berry, David James Duncan, Robert Frost, A. Bartlett Giamatti, E. B. White, P. D. James, Julian of Norwich, Garret Keizer, Tracy Kidder, Anne Lamott, May Sarton.
6 x 9, 320 pp, 5 b/w illus., Quality PB, 978-1-59473-118-1 **$18.99**
HC, 978-1-59473-005-4 **$22.99**

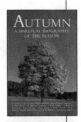

Spring: A Spiritual Biography of the Season
Edited by Gary Schmidt and Susan M. Felch; Illustrations by Mary Azarian
Explore the gentle unfurling of spring and reflect on how nature celebrates rebirth and renewal. Includes Jane Kenyon, Lucy Larcom, Harry Thurston, Nathaniel Hawthorne, Noel Perrin, Annie Dillard, Martha Ballard, Barbara Kingsolver, Dorothy Wordsworth, Donald Hall, David Brill, Lionel Basney, Isak Dinesen, Paul Laurence Dunbar.
6 x 9, 352 pp, 6 b/w illus., HC, 978-1-59473-114-3 **$21.99**

Summer: A Spiritual Biography of the Season
Edited by Gary Schmidt and Susan M. Felch; Illustrations by Barry Moser
"A sumptuous banquet.... These selections lift up an exquisite wholeness found within an everyday sophistication."— ★ *Publishers Weekly* starred review
Includes Anne Lamott, Luci Shaw, Ray Bradbury, Richard Selzer, Thomas Lynch, Walt Whitman, Carl Sandburg, Sherman Alexie, Madeleine L'Engle, Jamaica Kincaid.
6 x 9, 304 pp, 5 b/w illus., HC, 978-1-59473-083-2 **$21.99**

Winter: A Spiritual Biography of the Season
Edited by Gary Schmidt and Susan M. Felch; Illustrations by Barry Moser
"This outstanding anthology features top-flight nature and spirituality writers on the fierce, inexorable season of winter.... Remarkably lively and warm, despite the icy subject." — ★ *Publishers Weekly* starred review.
Includes Will Campbell, Rachel Carson, Annie Dillard, Donald Hall, Ron Hansen, Jane Kenyon, Jamaica Kincaid, Barry Lopez, Kathleen Norris, John Updike, E. B. White.
6 x 9, 288 pp, 6 b/w illus., Deluxe PB w/flaps, 978-1-893361-92-8 **$18.95**
HC, 978-1-893361-53-9 **$21.95**

Spirituality / Animal Companions

Blessing the Animals: Prayers and Ceremonies to Celebrate God's Creatures, Wild and Tame *Edited by Lynn L. Caruso* 5 x 7¼, 256 pp, HC, 978-1-59473-145-7 **$19.99**

What Animals Can Teach Us about Spirituality: Inspiring Lessons from Wild and Tame Creatures *by Diana L. Guerrero* 6 x 9, 176 pp, Quality PB, 978-1-893361-84-3 **$16.95**

Spirituality

Awakening the Spirit, Inspiring the Soul
30 Stories of Interspiritual Discovery in the Community of Faiths
Edited by Brother Wayne Teasdale and Martha Howard, MD; Foreword by Joan Borysenko, PhD
Thirty original spiritual mini-autobiographies showcase the varied ways that people come to faith—and what that means—in today's multi-religious world.
6 x 9, 224 pp, HC, 978-1-59473-039-9 **$21.99**

The Alphabet of Paradise: An A–Z of Spirituality for Everyday Life
by Howard Cooper 5 x 7¼, 224 pp, Quality PB, 978-1-893361-80-5 **$16.95**

Creating a Spiritual Retirement: A Guide to the Unseen Possibilities in Our Lives
by Molly Srode 6 x 9, 208 pp, b/w photos, Quality PB, 978-1-59473-050-4 **$14.99**
HC, 978-1-893361-75-1 **$19.95**

Finding Hope: Cultivating God's Gift of a Hopeful Spirit
by Marcia Ford 8 x 8, 200 pp, Quality PB, 978-1-59473-211-9 **$16.99**

The Geography of Faith: Underground Conversations on Religious, Political and Social Change *by Daniel Berrigan and Robert Coles* 6 x 9, 224 pp, Quality PB, 978-1-893361-40-9 **$16.95**

God Within: Our Spiritual Future—As Told by Today's New Adults *Edited by Jon M. Sweeney and the Editors at SkyLight Paths* 6 x 9, 176 pp, Quality PB, 978-1-893361-15-7 **$14.95**

Sacred Texts—SkyLight Illuminations Series

Offers today's spiritual seeker an accessible entry into the great classic texts of the world's spiritual traditions. Each classic is presented in an accessible translation, with facing pages of guided commentary from experts, giving you the keys you need to understand the history, context and meaning of the text. This series enables you, whatever your background, to experience and understand classic spiritual texts directly, and to make them a part of your life.

CHRISTIANITY

The End of Days: Essential Selections from Apocalyptic Texts—Annotated & Explained *Annotation by Robert G. Clouse*
Helps you understand the complex Christian visions of the end of the world.
5½ x 8½, 192 pp, Quality PB, 978-1-59473-170-9 **$16.99**

The Hidden Gospel of Matthew: Annotated & Explained
Translation & Annotation by Ron Miller
Takes you deep into the text cherished around the world to discover the words and events that have the strongest connection to the historical Jesus.
5½ x 8½, 272 pp, Quality PB, 978-1-59473-038-2 **$16.99**

The Lost Sayings of Jesus: Teachings from Ancient Christian, Jewish, Gnostic and Islamic Sources—Annotated & Explained
Translation & Annotation by Andrew Phillip Smith; Foreword by Stephan A. Hoeller
This collection of more than three hundred sayings depicts Jesus as a Wisdom teacher who speaks to people of all faiths as a mystic and spiritual master.
5½ x 8½, 240 pp, Quality PB, 978-1-59473-172-3 **$16.99**

Philokalia: The Eastern Christian Spiritual Texts—Selections Annotated & Explained *Annotation by Allyne Smith; Translation by G. E. H. Palmer, Phillip Sherrard and Bishop Kallistos Ware*
The first approachable introduction to the wisdom of the Philokalia, which is the classic text of Eastern Christian spirituality.
5½ x 8½, 240 pp, Quality PB, 978-1-59473-103-7 **$16.99**

Spiritual Writings on Mary: Annotated & Explained
Annotation by Mary Ford-Grabowsky; Foreword by Andrew Harvey
Examines the role of Mary, the mother of Jesus, as a source of inspiration in history and in life today. 5½ x 8½, 288 pp, Quality PB, 978-1-59473-001-6 **$16.99**

The Way of a Pilgrim: Annotated & Explained
Translation & Annotation by Gleb Pokrovsky; Foreword by Andrew Harvey
This classic of Russian spirituality is the delightful account of one man who sets out to learn the prayer of the heart, also known as the "Jesus prayer."
5½ x 8½, 160 pp, Illus., Quality PB, 978-1-893361-31-7 **$14.95**

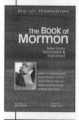

MORMONISM

The Book of Mormon: Selections Annotated & Explained
Annotation by Jana Riess; Foreword by Phyllis Tickle
Explores the sacred epic that is cherished by more than twelve million members of the LDS church as the keystone of their faith.
5½ x 8½, 272 pp, Quality PB, 978-1-59473-076-4 **$16.99**

NATIVE AMERICAN

Native American Stories of the Sacred: Annotated & Explained
Retold & Annotated by Evan T. Pritchard
Intended for more than entertainment, these teaching tales contain elegantly simple illustrations of time-honored truths.
5½ x 8½, 272 pp, Quality PB, 978-1-59473-112-9 **$16.99**

Sacred Texts—cont.

GNOSTICISM

The Gospel of Philip: Annotated & Explained
Translation & Annotation by Andrew Phillip Smith; Foreword by Stevan Davies
Reveals otherwise unrecorded sayings of Jesus and fragments of Gnostic mythology.
5½ x 8½, 160 pp, Quality PB, 978-1-59473-111-2 **$16.99**

The Gospel of Thomas: Annotated & Explained
Translation & Annotation by Stevan Davies Sheds new light on the origins of Christianity and portrays Jesus as a wisdom-loving sage. 5½ x 8½, 192 pp, Quality PB, 978-1-893361-45-4 **$16.99**

The Secret Book of John: The Gnostic Gospel—Annotated & Explained
Translation & Annotation by Stevan Davies The most significant and influential text of the ancient Gnostic religion. 5½ x 8½, 208 pp, Quality PB, 978-1-59473-082-5 **$16.99**

JUDAISM

The Divine Feminine in Biblical Wisdom Literature
Selections Annotated & Explained
Translation & Annotation by Rabbi Rami Shapiro; Foreword by Rev. Cynthia Bourgeault, PhD
Uses the Hebrew books of Psalms, Proverbs, Song of Songs, Ecclesiastes and Job, Wisdom literature and the Wisdom of Solomon to clarify who Wisdom is.
5½ x 8½, 240 pp, Quality PB, 978-1-59473-109-9 **$16.99**

Ethics of the Sages: Pirke Avot—Annotated & Explained
Translation & Annotation by Rabbi Rami Shapiro Clarifies the ethical teachings of the early Rabbis. 5½ x 8½, 192 pp, Quality PB, 978-1-59473-207-2 **$16.99**

Hasidic Tales: Annotated & Explained
Translation & Annotation by Rabbi Rami Shapiro
Introduces the legendary tales of the impassioned Hasidic rabbis, presenting them as stories rather than as parables. 5½ x 8½, 240 pp, Quality PB, 978-1-893361-86-7 **$16.95**

The Hebrew Prophets: Selections Annotated & Explained
Translation & Annotation by Rabbi Rami Shapiro; Foreword by Zalman M. Schachter-Shalomi
Focuses on the central themes covered by all the Hebrew prophets.
5½ x 8½, 224 pp, Quality PB, 978-1-59473-037-5 **$16.99**

Zohar: Annotated & Explained   *Translation & Annotation by Daniel C. Matt*
The best-selling author of *The Essential Kabbalah* brings together in one place the most important teachings of the Zohar, the canonical text of Jewish mystical tradition.
5½ x 8½, 176 pp, Quality PB, 978-1-893361-51-5 **$15.99**

EASTERN RELIGIONS

Bhagavad Gita: Annotated & Explained   *Translation by Shri Purohit Swami*
Annotation by Kendra Crossen Burroughs Explains references and philosophical terms, shares the interpretations of famous spiritual leaders and scholars, and more.
5½ x 8½, 192 pp, Quality PB, 978-1-893361-28-7 **$16.95**

Dhammapada: Annotated & Explained   *Translation by Max Müller and revised by*
Jack Maguire; Annotation by Jack Maguire Contains all of Buddhism's key teachings.
5½ x 8½, 160 pp, b/w photos, Quality PB, 978-1-893361-42-3 **$14.95**

Rumi and Islam: Selections from His Stories, Poems, and Discourses—
Annotated & Explained   *Translation & Annotation by Ibrahim Gamard*
Focuses on Rumi's place within the Sufi tradition of Islam, providing insight into the mystical side of the religion. 5½ x 8½, 240 pp, Quality PB, 978-1-59473-002-3 **$15.99**

Selections from the Gospel of Sri Ramakrishna: Annotated & Explained
Translation by Swami Nikhilananda; Annotation by Kendra Crossen Burroughs
Introduces the fascinating world of the Indian mystic and the universal appeal of his message. 5½ x 8½, 240 pp, b/w photos, Quality PB, 978-1-893361-46-1 **$16.95**

Tao Te Ching: Annotated & Explained   *Translation & Annotation by Derek Lin*
Foreword by Lama Surya Das Introduces an Eastern classic in an accessible, poetic and completely original way. 5½ x 8½, 192 pp, Quality PB, 978-1-59473-204-1 **$16.99**

About SKYLIGHT PATHS Publishing

SkyLight Paths Publishing is creating a place where people of different spiritual traditions come together for challenge and inspiration, a place where we can help each other understand the mystery that lies at the heart of our existence.

Through spirituality, our religious beliefs are increasingly becoming a part of our lives—rather than *apart* from our lives. While many of us may be more interested than ever in spiritual growth, we may be less firmly planted in traditional religion. Yet, we do want to deepen our relationship to the sacred, to learn from our own as well as from other faith traditions, and to practice in new ways.

SkyLight Paths sees both believers and seekers as a community that increasingly transcends traditional boundaries of religion and denomination—people wanting to learn from each other, *walking together, finding the way.*

For your information and convenience, at the back of this book we have provided a list of other SkyLight Paths books you might find interesting and useful. They cover the following subjects:

Buddhism / Zen	Gnosticism	Mysticism
Catholicism	Hinduism /	Poetry
Children's Books	Vedanta	Prayer
Christianity	Inspiration	Religious Etiquette
Comparative	Islam / Sufism	Retirement
Religion	Judaism / Kabbalah /	Spiritual Biography
Current Events	Enneagram	Spiritual Direction
Earth-Based	Meditation	Spirituality
Spirituality	Midrash Fiction	Women's Interest
Global Spiritual	Monasticism	Worship
Perspectives		